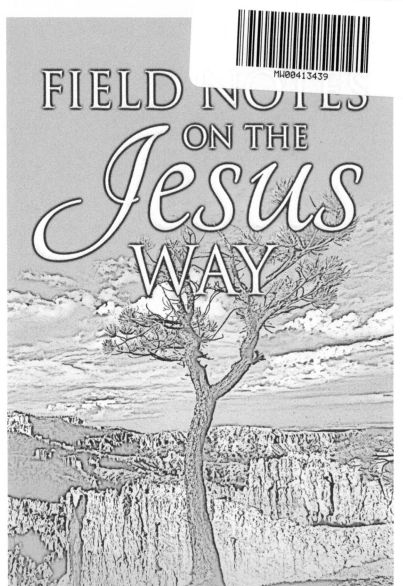

FIELD NOTES
ON THE
Jesus
WAY

JOE CHAMBERS

Field Notes on The Jesus Way
  By Joe Chambers

ISBN: 9781673603040

Field Notes
On The
Jesus Way

Paul & Aroli;

Goce and peace to you.
Remember who you are!
Deut. 33:12

Joe

By
Joe Chambers

Acknowledgments

When I thought about who has helped me with the words found in this little book, too many names came to mind to list. But a few floated to the surface due to their faithful feedback to my writing. I want to thank my mother Earlene Chambers who has always been my most fierce and faithful encourager in pursuing this form of communication. My friend Russ Stark reads every single blog article I post. If I ever wonder if anyone is reading, I can always be certain Russ will read my words. Cameron Crabtree has often been able to reduce an entire essay into a sentence or a phrase, and that has motivated me to tell the truth. Jamie Greening is my writing hero. His discipline and way with words are what I want to be when I grow up.

Folks who have had a hand in editing and giving feedback are Tina Tremain, Lisa Witcher, Robbie Boyd, Kirsten Yanasak, Danielle Pettibone, Helen Presswood, Karen Heise, and Tina Braswell—I am so very grateful to you all.

Introduction

I stand 6'4" and weigh over two hundred pounds but felt physically insignificant standing next to David. He weighed north of four hundred pounds and was one of my first baptisms in my first church—almost three decades ago. When we both stood in the baptismal, we displaced a goodly amount of water. The choir seemed a little nervous as two behemoths stepped into the water behind them, for the only thing between them and a biblical flood was an 8-inch tall pane of glass.

I faced the congregation and David faced my left. I told him that he would have to bend his knees and help me get himself back up after he was fully immersed. He nodded and licked his dry lips like he was nervous. As it turns out, there was good reason for both of us to be nervous.

I wore fishing waders underneath my snow-white Baptismal robe. David was dressed in a blue shirt and "overhauls"—4XL. He folded his hands together at the surface of the water, ready to clasp his nose as I tipped him back for a full dunking. I put my right hand in the middle of his back, between his shoulder blades and raised my left hand, palm facing out toward the congregation, and began to recite the familiar incantation: "David, upon your profession of faith and in obedience to the commands of our Lord and Savior, I now baptize my brother in the name of the Father, the Son and the Holy Spirit."

His hands went to his face and clinched his nose as water ran down his elbows. He bent his knees and began to lean back. I spread my feet and prepared for his weight in my strong right hand. But it wasn't strong enough, even with the help of the buoyancy of water. When he passed some sort of geometric tipping point, he went down into the water like a sack of stones. There was nothing I could do but get out of his way.

As he went under, fear set in and David's hands left his face. He began flailing for something to grab to save himself from going to the bottom. Not once or twice, but at least three times he groped and grabbed at me, the curtains—anything—while his bare feet tried to get purchase on the slick concrete floor.

Heads in the choir turned with furrowed brows of concern upon hearing the thrashing just feet away. One later said to me that he couldn't tell if I was trying to help or kill him. Everyone's eyes got as large as offering plates when David's ham hock of a hand landed on and tightly gripped the only thing standing between them and Noah's flood. He had grabbed the glass with his right hand and my robe with his left and was trying to right himself, spitting and spewing water out of flared nostrils like a surfacing beluga whale.

I went low and dead-lifted with all my might so as to take pressure off the glass and thus save the lives of men and women in the choir that tithed regularly. Somehow, with the strength of Samson, I lifted David and spared all from the flood. As he stood and wiped the water from his eyes, tsunami waves slapped from one end of the tank to the other. The choir released a collective sigh and someone muttered, I think it was Otis Whittington, "That was as close to dying in church service as I have ever come."

David climbed out with effort. He was winded. I was too. After we dried off he confided in me that the reason he wanted to be baptized in our church was because he thought I was the only preacher in the county who was large enough and strong enough to handle him. Then he said something that I have never forgotten. Layered with meaning he said, "Pastor, everything was going great until you let me down."

In the pages that follow, you will find a man who has let folks down and left them gasping for air. But this man has also been visited by the Lord and invited to eat breakfast at a restoration fire. The ministry of restoration has been around a long time. Without restoration, Moses would have been a shepherd the rest of his life. Without restoration, Elijah would still be pouting under a broom tree, David would never have written some of his best Psalms, and Jonah would have been fish poop on the bottom of the Mediterranean Sea. Without restoration, Peter would have finished his days fishing and John Mark would have never written one of our Gospels.

I invite you to walk with me and listen for an echo of grace that is Heaven-bent on restoring this world one heart at a time.

> *Dear Lord,*
>
> *I remember when I stepped into the pool of cold water at age seven with my father. There was a concrete block on the bottom for me to stand on and various pieces of trash floating on the surface. I remember being fearful of stepping off the block and going in over my head, but I also remember the strong hands of my father around my shoulders as he dipped me down into the water. I remember his voice pronouncing a blessing and feeling completely safe in his arms. I am grateful that, through the years of sin-flotsam in my life the constant has always been Your strong arm and voice of grace assuring me that no matter the depth of trouble—You will always lift me up. Amen.*

"One of the great sorrows, which came to human beings when Adam and Eve left the Garden, was the loss of memory, memory of all that God's children are meant to be." ~ Madeleine L'Engle

"Human beings are the only creatures trying to run away from home and to home at the same time."

~ John Ortberg

Part One:

Notes from the Wilderness...

"Thousands of tired, nerve-shaken, over-civilized people are beginning to find out going to the mountains is going home; that wilderness is a necessity..." ~ John Muir

"And this is what happened, and this is why the caribou and the wolf are one; for the caribou feeds the wolf, but it is the wolf that keeps the caribou strong." ~ Farley Mowat

"And there came a voice from heaven, saying, Thou art my beloved Son, in whom I am well pleased. And immediately the spirit driveth him into the wilderness." ~ St. Mark

In life and in Webster, wilderness always precedes wisdom.

Beautiful Wild

In the beginning God created...

~ Genesis 1:1

Each of us has had moments in our lives when we've seen something in nature that stirs something in us. Nature has a very powerful way of reconnecting us to God as Creator. Most of us have had experiences in nature where we have felt that staggering sense of complexity and diversity, breathtaking beauty, astonishing creativity, and added to all of that, the joy of discovery we have in that moment.

I grew up living at 9,000 feet above sea level in the mountains of Colorado. For some perspective, Mt. Baker in Washington stands 10,781 feet. In the mountains, I always felt cradled in the very hands of God. I remember mountain meadows of wild flowers with more colors than a Monet landscape. My brother and I spent summer nights camping without a tent in the crisp night air at that high altitude, gazing up at the skies. We watched as shooting stars streaked across the obsidian sky, leaving moments of light that looked like phosphorus strands of angel hair. Sunsets splash those mountains with an alpine glow of pink turning them crimson right before our eyes. My father told me it was that blood-red hue at sunrise and sunset that caused Spanish conquistadors to give the mountains their name hundreds of years ago: Sangre De Cristo, or Blood of Christ.

The lush forests in the Quinault Valley, located in the Olympic National Forest of Washington state, are some of the most spectacular examples of primeval temperate rain forest in the lower forty-eight states. Storms off the Pacific Ocean drop between twelve to fourteen feet of rain every year. You read that right: Feet. Epiphytes, or plants growing on other plants, mosses, spike mosses, ferns, and lichens, festoon tree trunks and branches give the forest a jungle-like feel. There are large old trees, the dominant species being Sitka spruce and western hemlock, but other conifers and several deciduous species grow as well. Many are hundreds of years old and can reach 250 feet in height and thirty to sixty feet in circumference.

There are so many things in our world that if we pause to take the time, will not only take our breath away and move us, but will cause us to be reconnected with something inside that is drawn to the God who created them. "God, who made the world and everything in it, since He is Lord of heaven and earth, does not dwell in temples made with hands…so that they should seek the Lord, in the hope that they might grope for Him and find Him, though He is not far from each one of us" (*New King James Version,* Acts 17: 24, 27).

There's something about creation that reminds us not only of the greatness and the creativity of God, but it reminds us that He is near…this God who made the world. Even David Hume, who was considered the father of modern skeptics, wrote that the whole frame of nature bespeaks an intelligent Author. I think we make a mistake in looking at the story of Genesis and trying to answer the HOW question of creation instead of the WHY question of creation.

"In the beginning God created the heavens and the earth" (Genesis 1:1). That ten-word sentence changed everything. And it tells me that, while infinitely distant from my Creator-God in degree, I am not as far away in kind. For I have been created in His image and this creation is the parchment upon which He is writing a story of grace, redemption, and restoration. He loves me, and this wild world tells me that at every turn.

Struggling for Repose

*When I am restored and rest in Thee, give me summer weather
in my heart.*

~ Heavenly Father, *The Valley of Vision*

My rainfly stretched taut under a Cypress tree. I washed
down a lovely dinner of chicken ramen with a piping hot cup of
lemon Gatorade. The sun slid behind the ridgeline, the light was
gauzy gray in the steep canyon. I sat beside the clear-running
south fork of the Sauk river journaling and nursing the hot
lemon drink while no-see-ums chewed away at my exposed
flesh. Small stones dislodged by the cold current thumped
along under water as they found a new resting place. Swallows
and bats patrolled the banks flitting for insects. I wrote in my
notebook: *I feel at rest here.* With the dull pain of hips bruised
from carrying the weight of my pack and feet sore from new
boots, I sat totally and eternally at rest.

The next morning I climbed the Weeden Creek trail to
Gothic Basin. The steep, rocky trail traverses the densely
wooded north-facing canyon wall. Towards the top of the
canyon rim the trail disappeared under a stubborn, late-summer
snow bank stretching vertically for hundreds of yards, sculpted
by sun and wind to form pock-marked caves. Cold air trapped
in the caves prickled my skin. A mile or so further, I came
across another steep snowfield with an underlying ice sheet. I
decided to find a flat spot of ground to spend the night. I could
see the glaciered valleys on the high mountains across the
canyon. Bare tree branches on scoured trunks sighed in the
gentle breeze. Heather bloomed a soft pink, like little orbs of
roe all along the trail. Back down the trail a few yards, I found
a good place to make camp with a water source about seventy-
five yards further down.

Normally I would never set up camp so close to the trail, but on this steep ascent the choices were limited.

Weather moved in and the next morning clouds shrouded the entire valley. Visibility was reduced to about fifty yards. I decided to wait out the weather before finding a way across the upper snowfield and finishing out at Foggy Lake up in Gothic Basin. Just off the trail I found a spider web suspended under an evergreen bow. Moisture from the dense fog caused water droplets to collect like little diamonds along the strands. The web's circular and woven structure adorned with these delicate jewels of moisture reminded me of a dream catcher. It was beautiful. I took several pictures with the camera on my phone. Feeling a surge of joy rise from a place deep in me, I put the phone in my pocket and jogged three steps on the wet grass back toward camp. It is what I feel when I hear a car pull up in my driveway and know it is my grandchildren coming to visit.

With the third giddy step my right foot slipped, contorting under me, heal pointing downhill, body facing cross-hill, twisting violently to my right; I slammed hard onto the ground. I heard a snap and felt an explosion of heat on the outside of my right leg just where the top of my boot might end had I been wearing them instead of my camp sandals. Pain shot up my leg as I wiggled my toes and shook my foot back and forth, causing me to gasp. I crawled hands-and-knees back to camp. Sitting on a rock and feeling nauseous, I broke out in a cold sweat. I peeled off my outer layers, put my head between my knees, and slowed down my breathing. The burning continued on my leg like someone was pouring a warm, fizzing liquid on my bare skin, letting it run down into my sock. I checked to see if it was blood . . . no.

I crawled under my shelter to catch my breath. The pain was not too bad until I moved my leg. I double-checked my phone for reception, but nothing had changed since the day before. I was alone with no way to contact anyone. My mind worked my options. Is it really broken or just a high ankle sprain? How could I tell? Water was a priority before my leg swelled up and

I couldn't put any weight on it. Crawling on all fours, I carefully kept my right foot several inches above the ground. My trekking pole would be my crutch. Standing, I put a little weight on it...not too bad. I took a step. "It is uncomfortable, but I can do this," I said out loud. Stepping awkwardly on the uneven ground, pain ripped up my leg and shot out my head like electricity. It would be a long walk.

An hour later I arrived back in camp and dropped my dromedary to the ground. I was breathless from the hellish climb down the trail to water. I crawled onto my Therm-a-Rest, pulled my sleeping bag over my back, and tried to calm my body down. Mosquitoes circled over my face like miniature buzzards over carrion. My leg throbbed with every beat of my heart, so I elevated it. Using my mental checklist, I considered food, water, clothing, and timelines of a possible rescue. My wife would call my friend, who knew where I was, when I was twenty-four hours late. I had enough food to last four or five days. I could get to water even though it would be painful. I was camped on a popular trail. Someone was likely to come walking by before I would be missed at home.

It was a cold night and I slept carefully, never very far from consciousness. The most painful moment I felt since the accident was crawling out in the morning and standing up to pee. My entire lower leg had swollen. Breakfast and coffee tasted good. The weather improved and the sun burned off the fog that had clung to the valley for the last twenty-four hours. I relaxed in the sunshine and waited. The face buzzards swirled around me as I tried to read a book; and I waited. Waiting always slows time.

Sometime early in the afternoon I saw movement out of my left eye. My hand reached for my Bear Spray. I had not kept as clean a camp as I might normally practice, but it wasn't a bear. It was a hiker. I yelled for him to come over to my camp. He froze, stooped down to get a better view of me lying under my low-slung rainfly. He walked slowly towards me. "I have hurt my leg," I said. He squatted at the edge of my shelter, a .40

caliber Glock 22 strapped to his waist. He was enjoying a day hike on his day off; he volunteered with Search and Rescue and had a radio. Boris spoke with a pronounced accent that sounded German, but he said he was from the Netherlands.

An hour later the Snohomish County Search and Rescue helicopter circled overhead. Boris packed up my gear. The rescuers repelled down from above the treetops. The first one came to me, put his hand on my shoulder, and said in a kind voice, "Everything is okay now. We will take good care of you and get you out of here." My chin quivered and my eyes stung with tears. They strapped me onto a litter board, wrapped me in a bright red fiberglass shroud, and grunted heavily as the three of them carried me twenty yards up to the evacuation area where the chopper hovered some two hundred feet above. I was helpless as I was being helped.

The cable attached to my litter grew taut and up into the blue sky I went as treetops glided by in my peripheral vision. I moved steadily towards the blades of the chopper with my hands strapped down by my side. I remember thinking this should be fun, but it was extremely unnerving, like being on an amusement ride when you change your mind and want off. There was no getting off. They wouldn't have heard me or let me off if they had. They were bent on rescuing me.

I broke my fibula. What surprised me in this experience was that I desperately wanted the benefits of being rescued yet found it very difficult to submit to the process of that rescue. Submitting and relinquishing was the only way out.

Lots of people, like me, would do well to find their rest in the Rescuer. Like children who fight sleep, we fight relinquishing our lives to the care and control of the only One who can give us the help we need. I have a stubborn and restless soul, and yet I have been designed to cooperate with the One who made me. After all, the first man, Adam, was created to walk and work with God in creation.

We have been struggling to get back to that Garden ever since.

King Jesus

Then Pilate asked Him, saying, "Are You the King of the Jews?" He answered him and said, "It is as you say." So Pilate said to the chief priests and the crowd, "I find no fault in this Man." But they were the more fierce, saying, "He stirs up the people..."

~ Luke 23:3-5

My faith claims that Jesus of Nazareth is King of the Universe. Part of me hates that idea. It forces me into an "all or nothing" decision. If He is King of kings, what does that make me? A subject, that's what. If Jesus were just a teacher pointing the way to a better life or a way to God, we could debate the philosophical merits and logic of his arguments. But in John 14:6 He says, "I am the way and the truth and the life. No one comes to the Father except through me" (*New International Version*). You can't be neutral about that. It is either true, He is a liar, or He is a nut job. We cannot "like" Jesus as if He were a Facebook comment. You have to dismiss and attack him or fall on your knees and call him King.

Earth is on the outer edge of the Milky Way. Light from stars on the opposite edge takes 100,000 years to reach us. That is fast. Our sun is one among 200 billion stars in our galaxy. Yet our galaxy is only one of 100+ billion galaxies in the observable universe. In the constellation Aquarius, one galaxy is believed to be 12 billion years old. That means it was born a relatively brief 2 billion years after the Big Bang. By comparison, our own solar system is quite young at 4.5 billion years old.

If you believe Jesus created all of that, you don't invite Him to be your assistant when life gets too messy. Jesus is not and never will be your life coach, helping you achieve your life goals. He is King. And what do you do for a King? Kneel.

I can't kneel now because of cartilage trauma. But before that I struggled with kneeling because of a hard heart. So do you. Do you ever see fingerprints around a "Wet Paint" sign? Something inside of us does not like anyone telling us what to do. At the core of our hearts something says, "Nobody tells me how to live!" If Jesus is just a teacher, I can weigh whether or not to receive His teachings. But if He is the third Person of the Trinity, if He is the Creator-God, if He is King, well, then I must do something altogether different.

> *Gentle Jesus, meek and mild,*
> *Look upon a little child;*
> *Pity my simplicity,*
> *Suffer me to come to Thee.*

That's a nice children's prayer, but there comes a day to put away childish things and as a full-grown man bow my knee and pray, "I will follow You the rest of my days, my Brother...my Captain...my King."

He doesn't leave another option.

Ugly Trees

I grew up at an elevation of 9,000 feet in Colorado, nine miles from town, and three miles from our nearest neighbor. One year my dad, brother, sister, and I went to the woods half a mile away to find our Christmas tree. We post-holed through the crusted snow from tree to tree. "How about this one, Dad?" Again and again he said no.

"But it's perfectly shaped," we would respond.

"Let's leave the pretty ones in the forest."

"Why, Dad?"

"So God can enjoy them in his forest," my dad replied.

Finally we heard, "Here it is." We groaned at the first sight of it. It was medium height, sparsely branched, and one side was almost bereft of branches. The crown drooped. The color was a pale green. The trunk was crooked as a dog's hind leg. "Perfect," Dad said. "Your mom can make it beautiful once we get it into the house." Down on his knees in the crunchy snow, he placed the bow saw against its bark and began to cut down the tree. I remember looking at my brother and sister with raised eyebrows. I think one of them said, "Mom's not going to like this."

I don't remember how my mom felt about the perfectly imperfect tree, but we all threw every ornament in the house on it. We turned the bareness towards the wall. We threw silver streaming icicles on the branches. We shredded cotton balls and threw them on the desperate needles for snow. Large baseball-sized globe ornaments went on the bottom and incrementally smaller ones towards the top. Egg-sized lights were strung all around. A star was placed at the bent crown. With an adjustment here and there and a final turn of the tree for the best angle in the family room, we were finished. "See? I told you," Dad said with a smile. "Beautiful."

I don't remember ever doing it that way again. My mom probably drew a line in the snow about bringing weeds into the house and passing them off as Christmas trees. I was associated with about twenty Christmas trees in my family as a boy growing up. I don't remember a single Christmas tree but this one.

The ordinary became extraordinary.

The ugly became beautiful.

The unwanted became wanted.

The obscure became remembered.

That can happen again this year in your home around your tree. The reason we celebrate gifts under a tree is because of another tree: a rough-sawn, blood-soaked tree. One no one wanted but is now treasured. Not because of its own intrinsic beauty, but because by dying on that ugly tree, Jesus made it beautiful.

> *On a hill far away stood an old rugged cross,*
> *The emblem of suff'ring and shame;*
> *And I love that old cross where the dearest and best*
> *For a world of lost sinners was slain.*

Linger at that ugly, ancient tree and receive your gift of acceptance, love, and hope.

Bears and Bread

Some folks drive the bears out of the wilderness
Some to see a bear would pay a fee
Me I just bear up to my bewildered best
And some folks even see the bear in me

~ Lyle Lovett

A few summers ago I took my son Caleb backpacking in Colorado. At that time he was sixteen and not altogether sure that he wanted to spend that much time alone with his dad. But I knew that in the culture of our family, it was important that he and I have some alone time in the wild. Almost none of our goals were realized in terms of destinations. The snow pack was too deep to get to the alpine lakes and the caves we wanted to explore. We were stuck in camp, lakes frozen over and caves filled with snow. Conversation was truncated and awkward. I wanted this experience to bond us together, but it was torturous. We don't share the same taste in music, reading, current events, or much of anything else. Wait, that is not true; we both love the same woman: his mom.

How do I connect with this guy?

One evening we were sitting on a log and finishing up supper when Caleb said in a low whisper, "Dad, look!" I looked up and about thirty yards away was a large cinnamon-colored bear walking through our meadow. He looked over at us and kept walking. I grabbed my video camera, but by the time I got it turned on and pointed in his direction, he was disappearing into the wooded edge of the meadow. I think I got five seconds of him on the camera. It was quite an adrenaline rush. We both were very pumped and quivering with excitement.

Then I noticed something. Before the bear came into our

world, Caleb was at the far end of the log whittling on a stick while his supper cooled. After the bear walked by, he had moved some eight feet towards me, sitting on the same log. In fact, he sat beside me on that log the rest of the night. He had been sulking a bit before the bear. He was missing his girlfriend, his mother, his X-box, and his bed. After the bear came through camp, he was not sulking anymore. He was fully present. He was "there" in the wilderness.

In the tent that night we both laughed and giggled at every snapped twig that sounded in the darkness. Once, just when he drifted to sleep, I rumbled a low growl and grabbed his leg. He screamed and hollered. We both split the night with laughter. Later he tried it on me and I screamed like Yogi and Boo-Boo were pulling me out of the tent. He laughed and laughed.

As I reflect on that time I wonder if it is possible that the Heavenly Father allows dangers into our world to do a couple of things: One, draw us closer to Him on the log and two, to cause us to be fully present where we are.

Is that why Jesus tells us to ask for "our daily bread" instead of our monthly bread?

Mosquito Man Pass

On a relief map
mountains remind my fingers:
"Where Crazy Horse tried."

~ William Stafford (Sioux Haiku)

One of us said, "What is that moving this way?" Someone reached for their spyglass and described what he saw. At 13,000 feet and walking towards us a half-mile away was a man with no backpack, raingear, or anything you might normally consider important while climbing the alpine ridges of the Sangre De Cristo mountain range in Colorado. But there he came as quick as you please.

He wore a floppy straw hat with a red bandanna wrapped around the sweatband. Some sort of cordage tied it under his chin. He was garbed in a plain white Fruit-of-the-Loom undershirt and sky-blue unhemmed polyester dress slacks cut off mid-thigh with stray strands blowing like spider webs in the breeze. He sported low-grade suede hiking shoes and white cotton athletic socks. Dangling from his leather belt was an almost empty gallon milk jug of drinking water.

As this was described to us, our mood moved from disbelief to confusion to incredulity. We had seventy-pound packs, $300 backpacking boots, and not a stitch of cotton on our bodies to guard against hypothermia. We had rain gear, rope, enough food for six days, water purification tablets, sleeping bags, emergency gear, and a first aid kit. We were totally prepared for these rugged mountains.

Not this guy. When he approached our resting and condescending group, he smiled and said, "Howdy!" His

13

glasses were thick and they fogged up as he looked at us. He barely breathed hard at this altitude. He scratched at his right forearm, then his neck, and then at his thigh. Someone asked where he was camped and he shrugged and tossed his head to his left down the line of ridges indicating south and said, "Back that-a-way."

"Where you headed?" we asked next.

With the same vagueness he jutted out his chin northward and said, "That-a-way."

We sat on a 13,200-foot pass where there was no trail; any viable campsite was hours away in any direction. If the mountains were a sea, we were atop a single wave with no landfall in sight. Where had this guy come from and where was he going?

He untwisted the lid to the milk jug and took a swallow of the little water that was left, wiped his mouth, and grinned. We were dumbstruck. He was dressed more like a beach bum from southern California than a man walking alpine ridges in Colorado. An awkward silence hung between us. Finally, someone asked him if he needed anything.

"I'm alright," he said. "Bugs are really bad, aren't they? I could use some insect repellent, if you could spare any." He was covered with pink bumps, some scabbed over, and some looked infected. Small pox or a hornets' nest was the first thing that came to my mind when I saw him standing there scratching.

My friend Jim jumped up and said, "I have a second bottle of Jungle Juice I'll give you."

"No. Just squirt me a little in this sandwich bag." He reached in his pocket pulled out a crumpled up baggie, turned it inside out dumping some crumbs, and held it open for Jim. About six or seven good squirts was enough, he said. He twisted a knot in the top of it and put it into his pocket, rubbed the spillage on his arms, legs, neck, and face.

"Don't get any of that juice on your glasses; it'll dissolve your lenses," someone offered. Nervous laughter rippled around our group in agreement.

"Well," he said. "I better get going. Thanks for the bug juice." He grinned, looked northward, and off he went. We watched him drop down over the edge of the ridge as if a rogue wave swamped him, never to be seen again.

Looking around at each other, checking for some clue of understanding at what we had witnessed, someone asked, "What just happened? Was that even real?"

If you look at a Crestone quadrangle topographical map, there is an unnamed ridge between Cleveland Peak and Tijeras Peak. That is where we saw him.

Do not forget to show hospitality to strangers,
for by so doing some people have shown hospitality
to angels without knowing it.

~ Hebrews 13:2

Smoke on the Trail

Hiking along the Pacific Crest Trail (PCT), you meet people who have trail names. These folks are usually "Through Hikers," meaning they started in Mexico and are headed for the Canadian border. "Section Hikers" are folks who have subdivided the PCT into large chunks like Oregon or Washington or large sections of California. Then there are "destination hikers" and "day hikers." I was a Section Hiker.

Almost all Through Hikers, and a few Section Hikers, had trail names like Bear Cow, Kindergarten Cop, Skinny D, Roger Dodger, and Sweet Jesus. Most names originated from some memorable event. "Bear Cow" got scared by glowing eyes at the edge of the firelight one night, convinced he was being stalked by a bear only to find out it was a cow. "Skinny D" is short for skinny dipper. "Sweet Jesus" is a kid with long hair and a beard like…Jesus. And, yes, I had a trail name. The ex-cop from L.A. learned I was a pastor and started calling me "The Rev." On the trail, as in other arenas, one of the first small-talk questions asked is "What do you do for a living?" It is one way we identify ourselves. I'm a pastor, policeman, or teacher. But is what you do really who you are down at the core? Is what you do the ultimate truth? What happens if I stop being a pastor? Who will I be then?

> In those days Jesus came from Nazareth of Galilee and was baptized by John in the Jordan. And just as he was coming up out of the water, he saw the heavens torn apart and the Spirit descending like a dove on him. And a voice came from heaven, "You are my Son, the Beloved; with you I am well pleased."
>
> (*New Revised Standard Version,* Mark 1:9-11)

Listen to those words. "You are my [...] Beloved; with you I am well pleased." You are the beloved of God. Don't those words sound wonderful? Do I dare hope that voice might speak to me? Haven't you wanted and wished it to be true?

The first week I hiked solo some fifty miles from Ashland, Oregon, to Fish Lake Resort. I picked up the first re-supply package, filled with Ramen, trail mix and other backpacking stuffs that I had mailed myself two weeks earlier. Foot-sore, dirty, hungry, and a little lonely, I carried my re-supply box two hundred yards to the designated PCT hiker's camp. I set the box down on a picnic table, took my pack off, and stretched out under a canopy of fir boughs. I was almost asleep when I heard the heavy footfall of what I assumed was another hiker.

A tall, lanky, gray-bearded man lumbered up, bowed low and with open arms said, "Welcome, sir, to your new home. We are all family here and anything I have is yours. Let me know if you need anything. On the trail they call me 'Smoke.'" He stuck out his left hand to shake mine. He kissed two fingers on his right hand, bumped his chest over his heart twice, pointed at me and walked a few yards away and crawled into his tent.

Over the next twenty-four hours I learned he was not a hiker. He hung out at the PCT camp because he had no place else to go. He picked up trash around the resort and sorted out the hiker box, where backpackers left foodstuffs they didn't want. I think he ate out of that box. He never completed a sentence and often finished a story or conversation with lines from movies or 70s rock song lyrics. His favorite rock and roller was Bob Seger. I told him my favorite Seger song was "Turn the Page." He said, "Thank you." Whether the gratitude was from entering into his passions or giving him credit for having good taste in music, I couldn't tell.

Smoke found a discarded, broken, toy fishing pole. He brought it back to camp and began to work on it. After an hour and a little of my duct tape, he felt it would pass inspection. He then went around asking every older resort member he could find if they had kids or grandkids so he could give the fishing pole to them.

He asked me what I did when I wasn't hiking. When I tell people I am a pastor, they change. Smoke smiled ear-to-ear. We had long discussions about the Bible as I took a rest day at this resort. Smoke would talk and talk, but he didn't speak in linear ways. He would start down a line of logic and split off to chase a different topic, like a beagle that has jumped a rabbit, eventually coming back to the trail, but you didn't really know where he'd been in the meantime. Listening to him you knew he was a kind and gentle man, wanted nothing from anyone, and offered what he had to anyone who came along. He wrote me a three-page letter confessing sins, a life of drug abuse, and rambling lyrics from old songs sprinkled with clips of Bible verses.

When I packed up to go, he was talking a mile a minute. I turned to him saying, "Smoke, would you mind if I prayed for you?"

He said, "I would count it a privilege if you would just remember my name from time-to-time down the trail, pastor."

I said, "Smoke, can I pray for you right now?" He nodded his head. I asked him if I could put my hand on his shoulder. He nodded his head. I began to pray and Smoke tilted his head back just slightly as if basking in the last warm rays of the afternoon sun. When I said, "In Jesus name, Amen," and opened my eyes, big wet tracks of tears were flowing down his pockmarked cheeks. I placed my hand on his chest and said, "Smoke, you have a good heart beating in this chest. God loves you very much."

He smiled and said, "Pastor, my name is Gary."

Soul Sustainability

The grass withers, the flower fades; but the word of our God will stand forever.

~ Isaiah 40:8

He has made everything beautiful in its time. Also He has put eternity in their hearts...

~ Ecclesiastes 3:11

On the Oregon section of the Pacific Crest Trail through the Cascade Mountains of central Oregon, I met a lot of very interesting people. People from different professions, socio-economic stations, and many foreign countries like Switzerland, Finland, Australia, Ireland, and Texas.

Megan was hiking with her dog, Zoe. She had long brown hair with strands of gray streaking through her braids. I came upon her sitting in the shade one afternoon trying to cool down in 93 degree heat reading a Steinbeck novel. We chatted about Mr. Steinbeck for a while and then I moved on.

Two hours later I was taking a break in the shade of a tree and I heard singing from up the trail. Not particularly good singing, but singing—the kind of singing you do when you have ear buds in and don't think anyone is within earshot. Not something you hear very often in the wilderness. It was Megan and Zoe hiking at a good clip down the trail towards me singing along with Alanis Morissette. She blushed, waved, and kept walking.

We kept meeting on the trail and having clips of conversations about life on the trail for about 60 miles. One time a few of us were stopped at a stream, and she mentioned that her father had dropped her off at the trailhead in northern

California. I asked her a typical male/father question, "What does your father think of you hiking the trail all by yourself?" She shot me a defiant look and asked, "What does your father think of you hiking the trail all by yourself?" I felt I might have offended her so I said, "He'd be jealous." She said, "Yeah, my dad is jealous too."

Another time I asked this hippy, bohemian, Californian girl what she did away from the trail. She said she was a Sustainable Transportation Planner and Program Developer for a small college in Monterrey, California.

"Huh?"

"I'm a Sustainable Transportation Planner and Program Developer for a small college" —spoken a little slower as if I couldn't keep up.

I smiled and said that is so cool. I asked her to tell me about her work.

She said, "I advocate a vision of a transportation system that reduces greenhouse gas emissions, moves the most people in the least space with the least energy, and promotes public health through exercise. I promote strategies for transit service, transit capital improvements, transportation demand management, automobile parking, pedestrian connectivity and safety, bicycle connectivity and safety, and way-finding."

"Oh," I said.

I learned more about the environment than Al Gore sitting on that log beside that stream. I kept affirming her work of stewarding the environment, and the more I affirmed her the more she talked, this Sustainable Transportation Planner and Program Developer from California.

Finally she sighed and said, "I want this earth to be alive and well long after I'm gone and I've dedicated my life to make that happen."

"How long do you think that this earth is going to last?" I asked.

"Not very long if we don't do our part," she said.

"I couldn't agree with you more, Megan. I think the law of

entropy is clearly at work. As you know it states that anything left to itself will become more disorganized and more random. Like my garage. If I don't clean it out and put everything away, after a while it becomes cluttered and disorganized. The universe acts in the same way.

The earth is not sustainable because the Universe is not sustainable. But we want it to be. I certainly want it to be. But the best minds this world has ever produced have said it will end one day. Our sun will one day go super nova and burn out. It will all end one day. I believe in doing everything we can to care for it, but ultimately it is fading away. There is an old Jewish proverb that says, 'the grass withers, the flower fades and surely the people are grass.'"

She stared at me and then said, "So, are you saying that I should not be trying to save the planet?"

"No! Keep doing it! We need you to do your best to sustain this good earth. I'm just saying that ultimately it is winding down. But you aren't. You will live forever."

"What do you mean?" she asked.

"Just as thirst proves that there is water and hunger proves that there is food, your passion for a sustainable earth proves that you have eternity in your heart. You long for significance, you long for sustainability. It is in your DNA, in fact it is deeper than that, Megan. You have sustainability in your soul. Taste the huckleberries at your feet, look at Mount Jefferson, and listen to that wood pecker rapping away on that tree…you are similar and yet you are very different. Another old proverb says, 'He has made everything beautiful in its time. Also He has put eternity in their hearts.'"

She blinked and asked, "Who are you, really?"

I smiled and said, "I'm a Soul Sustainability Transportation Consultant and Program Developer for a small group of apprentices in Washington State."

She just blinked at me.

"I'm just messing with you, Megan. But I do work hard to awaken the sustainable. I hope you will continue to do your good work and listen to what your soul is trying to tell your head."

"Okay," she said. "Do you have any extra coffee?"

That was her signal that she was ready to change the topic. We said our goodbyes and I never saw her again.

Dallas Willard reminds us, "You are an unceasing spiritual being with an eternal destiny in God's great universe." This is just true, but I'm also like grass. I'm going to die. You're going to die. God didn't plant death in the human heart.. Death came because of sin, and that includes my sin, and I'm going to have to face a holy God on a day of reckoning, and I have not lived up to the standard of his holiness. Not by a million light-years. Human self-sufficiency is not going to get me out of this one. All the king's horses and all the king's men; all the creativity and pride of America is not going to innovate us out of this one.

That's why Jesus said, "For God so loved the world that He gave His only begotten Son, that whoever believes in Him should not perish but have everlasting life" (*New King James Version,* John 3:16). So, I listen to that divine echo of eternity in my soul and believe. In fact, I am doing more than that. I'm wagering my eternity on that echo. How about you?

Here's praying I see you on the other side.

Drama in the King's Chamber

Fatigue makes cowards of us all.

~ Vince Lombardi

Local legend has it that Spanish conquistadors used the passages in Colorado's Marble Caves to secret gold from one valley to the next. Having been in the caves, I highly doubt that. It is more than a little difficult just to get yourself through the tight passages, much less with a payload. The caves were discovered in the 1880s by a man who described them in 1888 as follows:

> Entrance to the cave is by a crevice in the rock, extending some 400 feet; upon entering one must crawl a distance of 25 feet; then, the investigator can walk in a stooping posture for 25 feet; next, a narrow passage is encountered through which only a person of small stature can pass; and finally a low passage is reached through which one gains entry to the King's Chamber.

Please note the phrase "only a person of small stature can pass." I am a very large man. It would be a challenge to take my sons into these caves at my age. Some places are so tight that I have to push all of the air out of my lungs and snake that part of my body through, and then suck my belly in and snake the rest of me through. Always put the fat guy first; if he gets stuck, only one is stuck. The other way around it is like a cork in the bottle, trapping everyone inside. That is an important lesson.

The approach was difficult due to living at sea level all year and sitting at a desk most of the time. The temperature was in the 80s and I struggled to stay hydrated. My two sons made it with ease. At the mouth of the cave we pulled on our wool gloves, hats, headlamps, and nylon wind pants to enter. I went first because I knew the way and am the largest by far, but mostly because I am the dad. I am strong that way. I am dominant that way.

We army-crawled through marmot scat and bat guano for several yards with grunts and huffs. My breathing was heavy. I heard the guys behind me making guttural noises as they squeezed through tight places like human toothpaste. At one point Caleb said to me breathlessly, "Dad, I am pretty impressed that you are making it through these tight places that are squeezing the life out of me." That made me feel good; then Clint muttered something about the malleability of fat.

At several points in the crawl, muscles began to cramp at the most inopportune time. I rued the water I had deprived myself of on our approach. We pushed, pulled, stretched, stooped, and inched our way onward towards the White Marble Hall, or as the 1888 article called it, the King's Chamber. I noticed my arms getting weaker and back muscles cramping. Stopping to catch our breath, we decided we had done the equivalent of over a hundred pushups. My arms quivered. I had not done any upper-body work in years. I was as soft as biscuit dough.

We crawled on in the cold. About 300 feet in I sat to rest. My heart started racing faster than normal. Looking ahead I saw tighter and tighter passages. My legs and back cramped and my arms quivered. I couldn't catch my breath. I can only describe it as panic. In a nanosecond I flashed on all my possible rescue scenarios and quickly concluded that no one could rescue me. No matter the injury, illness or hypothermia, the only person who could get me out was me. Could I wait for the guys to finish and crawl out with them? The heaving in my chest said no. Fear crept up on me. It started in my toes and rose up through my body and settled like a bully on my chest.

I said aloud, "I need to pray." The guys got quiet.

Instinctively I began to pray, "The Lord is my shepherd…" I breathed deeply and slowly and prayed some more. The bully pounded on my chest. It is hard to look weak in front of your sons and I was grateful for the darkness so they couldn't see my face flushed and embarrassed. Finally fear eclipsed shame and I said, "I have to get out. You guys can come with me or go on to the White Halls." They both agreed to go on. I started snaking my way out.

"I shall not want. He maketh me to lie down in green pastures." In five short minutes of crawling I stopped to listen for their grunts and moans. Silence. They were gone. I was alone. The bully started on me again and I crawled on. Then I began to imagine all that could go wrong for them; that I would be out and safe, and they would die in the cave. They had never done anything like this before. The bully was kicking my butt all the way out of the cave. Finally, I said to myself or God said to me…I couldn't tell which due to the bully, but these words came to my mind, "Trust your sons. They are men."

Surprisingly I got out a lot faster than it took to get in. Adrenalin is my favorite drug. The light blinded me and I blinked several times to adjust my eyes to the brightness. Chilled, I sat in the warm sun and fell asleep waiting for them. An hour later they came crawling and squinting out of the mouth of the cave. Clinton described shimmying up slick narrow walls like you would climb up the inside of a chimney. At one point he got scared and he kept saying over and over, "I can do this. I can do this."

As I reflected on the experience in the cave with the bully of fear and my plea for Jesus to help me, I began to think maybe I didn't have enough faith to overcome the bully. I started to crash and question the sincerity of my faith. On the trail a couple of days later, I was pouting over the cave incident and it was as if Jesus said to me, "Hey, Joe, did it ever occur to you that I did speak to you in the cave?"

"How so, Lord?"

"Get out!"

Unbearable Beauty

Beauty is unbearable, drives us to despair, offering us for a minute the glimpse of an eternity that we should like to stretch out over the whole of time.

~ Albert Camus

Never lose an opportunity of seeing anything beautiful, for beauty is God's handwriting.

~ Ralph Waldo Emerson

It is so easy to get sad. Just pay attention to what mankind is doing in and to the world, from the anemic economy to the chemical weapons in Syria, to the toddler tantrums in Washington, to the gray skies, and the fact that I burned my toast this morning. Sometimes it seems that we look for reasons to get our heads down and when we don't see a reason right away, we create a reason. What will help me with the ugliness all around? In a word, Beauty.

The earliest European cave paintings date some 32,000 years ago. The purpose of the Paleolithic cave paintings is not known. The evidence suggests that they were not merely decorations of living areas, since the caves in which they have been found do not have signs of ongoing habitation. Also, they are often in areas of caves that are not easily accessed. Some theories hold that they may have been a way of communicating with others, while other theories ascribe them a religious or ceremonial purpose. May I suggest another reason for the art? Man was created in the image of a Creator-God. And our Creator-God is an artist. Man was imitating his Creator 32,000 years ago. He still is.

King David was an artist and penned these words in Psalms

27:4:

> One thing I have desired of the Lord,
> That will I seek:
> That I may dwell in the house of the Lord
> All the days of my life,
> To behold the beauty of the Lord.
>
> *(New King James Version)*

Why do we need beauty? The answer to that question is found in the setting of Psalms 27—"For in the time of trouble"—verse 5. What trouble? Look in verses 2 and 3:

> When the wicked came against me
> To eat up my flesh,
> My enemies and foes,
> They stumbled and fell.

Though an army may encamp against me.

David was an ancient king. Armies muster all the time trying to dethrone rival kings. There was very little national security for David and his people. We do not know the insecurity that many nations feel all the time because they are surrounded by their enemies. The closest example to national insecurity we know was the aftermath following Pearl Harbor and 9/11.

My mother told me that this Psalm is special to her because as a young mother of three toddlers, while my dad was working nights and going to school during the day, she would feel vulnerable because of the unsafe neighborhood in which we lived. This Psalm comforted a young mother alone in a dangerous place.

Maybe these days your insecurities have to do with health, or your job, or a shaky relationship. Any problem can be an enemy of your life and soul. What I like about the Bible in general, and this Psalm in particular, is that it doesn't play silly mind games with believers about the difficulty of living in this sin-filled world. I agree with the quote from the Pulitzer award-winning author, Ernest Becker, who wrote, "I think that taking life seriously means something such as this: that whatever man does on this planet has to be done in the lived truth of the terror of creation, of the grotesque, of the rumble of panic underneath everything. Otherwise it is false."

In other words, to pretend that all of life is puppy breath, cotton candy, and Hallmark movies is not living in the real world. We are not taking life seriously unless we admit "the rumble of panic that lies underneath everything."

That is what this Psalm does. In verses 5 and 6, David is saying that whatever beholding the beauty of God means must include living with eyes wide open to the evil and falseness of this dark world.

> For in the time of trouble
> He shall hide me in His pavilion;
> In the secret place of His tabernacle
> He shall hide me;
> He shall set me high upon a rock.
> And now my head shall be lifted up above my
>   enemies all around me.

By beholding the beauty of God, David was able to strengthen himself and keep his head up, even though he was surrounded by enemies. David is not hiding, masking, or medicating his pain and trouble—his enemies are all around him. Yet, because he is beholding the beauty of God, his head is up. This isn't about just coping, sort of a grit your teeth and bear it; it is a way of having victory over them! He says, "My head shall be lifted above my enemies."

Beholding the beauty of God enables you and me to face "the rumble of panic underneath everything." The evil and terror of life in this dark world will not go away, but you and I will be able to live with our heads held high. It may be easy to get sad, but we are not bereft of a way to live: "Behold the beauty of the Lord."

Unforgettable

And I will give him a white stone, and on the stone a new name

~ Jesus, Revelation 2:17

There is a flower that lives above tree line in the Rocky Mountains that has captured my heart for almost 40 years. It is a flower that can be difficult to find. I shudder at the thought of how many times I might have trampled this raindrop-size flower under the rugged sole of my boot and have been none-the-wiser.

I've sat at 13,000 feet, chest heaving, trying to gasp every ounce of oxygen out of the thin air and, while on that tawny carpet of alpine tundra, head between my knees choking back mountain sickness, spied the Lilliputian pinwheel of blue petals and yellow pistils smiling at me in the shadow of my size 14 Asolo hiking boots. They come from the genus Myosotis, which in Greek, means "mouse ear." In a German legend, God named all the plants when a tiny unnamed one cried out, "Forget-me-not, O Lord!" God replied, "That shall be your name." Because the alpine forget-me-not flourishes on the tundra where the winter wind and snow blow with a fierce intensity, they never grow larger than the top button on your shirt.

In all my years of trekking at altitude I am filled with wonder when I find this shy flower. And each time I kneel down to get a closer look I whisper something that only God would hear. What has struck me over the years has been how such delicate beauty could survive in such harsh conditions, and I marvel at a Creator-God who would plant it in such inaccessible places. I have no idea how many times I have found the flower and thought God is delighting in his creation. Or to paraphrase Anne

29

Lamott, "God is showing off."

Showing off to whom? I would be the only person to see it. How many millions of little blue, mouse-eared flowers are never seen by any sentient earth-bound beings? He must have made those for His own delight. This is so unlike me. I do virtually nothing for the sake of beauty alone. I never prepare a sermon and want to preach it to an empty church. I never write an essay or a story hoping no one will ever read it. Any beauty I might try to create, I want to share with others. I want someone to say something laudatory about my so-called art. But my ego is fragile and I am trying to be larger than I am.

Each flower is the same. Doesn't God get weary of the sameness of His creation, no matter how heart-poundingly beautiful it might be? I guess the short answer is, "No." He keeps on doing it season after season, mountain after mountain, flower after flower.

Monotony is my enemy. Because I have sinned, monotony places me vulnerable to sin. Monotony caused King David to look at a bathing beauty. Monotony made the Pharisees fail to see the Creator-God walking and recreating in their very midst. I fear monotony. I fill my life with ear pollution, eye noise, and trivial pursuits.

Not God.

> Because children have abounding vitality, because they are in spirit fierce and free, therefore they want things repeated and unchanged. They always say, 'Do it again'; and the grown-up person does it again until he is nearly dead. For grown-up people are not strong enough to exult in monotony. But perhaps God is strong enough to exult in monotony. It is possible that God says every morning, 'Do it again' to the sun; and every evening, 'Do it again' to the moon. It may not be automatic necessity that makes all daisies alike; it may be that God makes every daisy separately, but has

never got tired of making them. It may be that He has the eternal appetite of infancy; for we have sinned and grown old, and our Father is younger than we. (G.K. Chesterton, *Orthodoxy*, page 108)

Beauty is a reminder of the "appetite of infancy" at the heart of our Creator-God. I find myself valuing it, wanting to possess it, and desiring to create it. There is something about beauty that takes us to the place of innocent delight of being a child. And perhaps it is in that wonder of delight we step into, if for but a moment—another garden coming down from heaven at the end of days.

So, you don't know my art? Perhaps you don't know my name. No matter. Each time I marvel at the beauty of a bashful flower, I remember that it is but a taste of another garden where I will receive my new name. Beauty reminds me that I am not forgotten. And neither are you.

Part Two:

Notes from Art

People see God every day, they just don't recognize him.

~ Pearl Bailey

All theology, like all fiction, is at its heart autobiography.

~ Frederick Buechner

Every happening, great and small, is a parable whereby God speaks

to us, and the art of life is to get the message.

~ Malcolm Muggeridge

The Peaceable Kingdom

The wolf shall live with the lamb... and a little child shall lead them.

~ Isaiah 11:6

There is a movie that I enjoyed a few years ago called "Grand Canyon." One of the characters in that film is an attorney named Mack, and he is locked in an L.A. traffic jam. He takes a short cut through a part of L.A. that is notorious for its street gangs. He moves deeper into bad neighborhoods until finally his fancy sports car stalls in a sketchy looking neighborhood.

Mack calls a tow truck, but before the truck could arrive a low-riding car with base-pounding music pulls up behind Mack's car. A group of neighborhood street thugs start piling out of that low-rider and move towards Mack and his nice car. They surround his car and begin to hassle him. Just about that time the tow truck pulls up and out steps an earnest, serious looking man named Simon (who is played by Danny Glover).

All of the street thugs start to protest and threaten both Mack and Simon, until Simon takes aside the leader of the street gang and says this:

> Man, the world ain't supposed to work like this. I mean, maybe you don't know that yet. I'm supposed to be able to do my job without having to ask you if I can. That dude is supposed to be able to wait with his car without you ripping him off. **Everything is supposed to be different than it is.**

That is a graduate ethics course on a street corner. Simon's street-side speech is a summary of what all of us experience in

35

this world. *Everything is supposed to be different than it is.* What we see on our news, what we see in our cities, what we see in our own community, and what we see in the mirror every morning is not the way it is supposed to be.

When you go to your kitchen faucet and fill a glass of tap water, and then turn on the news to learn that every year in our world 3.4 million people die of simple, curable water related diseases…you might think to yourself, *Everything is supposed to be different than it is.*

When you think about the fact that most of us grew up in a family that supported your education experience so that you can read, write, and do basic math— you will have exponentially more opportunities in life than many of the kids that grow up in inner cities like Denver and Dallas. If you are honest you will say to yourself, *Everything is supposed to be different than it is.*

When you open the first pages of the book that we love, we see a story of a Creator who fashions the cosmos, galaxies, worlds and a human family that is deeply good. God creates the world as an interwoven tapestry of relationships and goodness that is woven together in beauty and delight.

God creates a world that is good, just, and kind. It is swollen with possibilities. But early in the story our primal parents turned their backs on our Creator. And as that happens the fabric of the tapestry of God's good creation is torn and begins to unravel. The unraveling that sin has brought into this world tears at families, societies, and even the molecular structure of creation itself. *Everything is supposed to be different than it is.*

No other approach to God is like the Christian story. Lots of other religions talk about God's compassion for the poor—but only the Christian story says God becomes poor. When Jesus came to us in that manger, God became the poor and the powerless. God suffers injustice to draw out its sting, undo its power, and begin the work of restoring his world.

As we see what God has done for the weak and poor in Jesus, we who follow him—if we follow him close enough for the dust of his sandals to get on our clothes—then we will follow him down into obscurity, weakness, and poverty. "If you want to do the works of the One who is high and lifted up, serve the ones who are low and leveled down" (Beth Moore).

This is why it is hard for some of us to understand why so many "Christians" are so supportive of policies in local, state, and national governments that seem to do so much harm to the poor and the powerless of our society. If we follow closely the Jesus described in Scriptures, He will lead us to places that He would go and do the work that he would do. Honestly, I'm not certain that is where the majority of Christians in America want to go. They want to stay insulated and away from the poor and marginalized.

It is customary for self-righteous preachers from pulpits and Christian celebrity wags on television to whine and complain about how commercialized and materialistic Christmas has become. The war on Christmas that so many are concerned about is about getting back the true meaning of Christmas that does not include materialism. But may I be so bold as to say that I think just the opposite is accurate? **Christmas is a very materialistic celebration.** Because the Christmas story is a narrative of a God who came to inhabit cells, sinews, and sinuses—and to do something about what is wrong with this material world.

What this means is that as we walk closer to our rabbi and Savior, we will learn how to have a more materialistic Christmas. Christmas is good news for this material world. And that means that you and I ought to be diligent about how we can address the tears of this world.

Maybe instead of singing "Have yourself a merry little Christmas" we could adapt those lyrics to say, *"Have yourself a materialistic little Christmas."*

How do we do that?

When you look at the life of Jesus, you don't see him standing up for the poor out of anger or paranoia, but out of the deep communion with the God he calls Father. Out of a deep interior life of love with the one he calls Abba. When you look at Jesus you see someone who is brim-full with God's Spirit; who delights in the presence of God. All of Jesus' preaching, teaching, and ministry come from those deep wells of communion with God in prayer.

We pray and then we act.

When you look at Jesus, you are actually looking at God getting dirt under his fingernails in the pain, suffering, and wrong of this world. And God invites us to be like Jesus and actually do something about the wrong and neglected in our community.

You could start by noticing a neighbor who looks lonely and begin a relationship with them. You could start by opening your home to someone who needs someone to talk to. Start somewhere, start small, and do something.

There is a "Now" that God has accomplished in Jesus in the manger in Bethlehem, but there is a tomorrow that is not here yet. Maybe you have seen the artist Edward Hicks' depiction of this scene in a painting called *The Peaceable Kingdom*. Edward Hicks was a 19th century Quaker minister and painter. During the course of life, he was fascinated by this vision of a healed world, and painted this vision at least 62 times.

As he painted that scene over and over again in his life, the painting morphed, as did his understanding of life in this world. Towards the end of his hard life, disillusionment began to creep into his faith so that one of the last versions of *The Peaceable Kingdom* shows a darker scene. The child is still there, but the animals have changed so that they all look more predatorial. Their claws are showing, and their fangs are bared.

If we are honest, you and I still live in a claws-out, fangs-bared kind of world. So, this "Not Yet" half of Isaiah's vision invites us to the discipline of waiting. I find it interesting that in our world that is allergic to waiting, we Christ-followers still have to endure bared fangs and claws as we look out our windows towards the eastern skies and wait for the coming of our Lord. That is the day when everything that is supposed to be different—is different.

In the meantime, we are called to wait now—for a great future in which God will make all things new. Waiting is holy not-doing. It is disciplined looking ahead with your mental and emotional energy, your imagination, and your deep yearnings for that **NOT YET** day.

And so, my friend I hope you have yourself a materialistic little Christmas this year.

Echoes of Eden

Blood Diamond is a powerful movie in which an African character named Solomon Vandy is in constant pursuit of his son, Dia, kidnapped by Revolutionary United Front (RUF) guerillas several weeks earlier. Solomon himself had been enslaved by the RUF and forced to work in the diamond fields. He finds a rare diamond worth millions and buries it, hoping he can "buy back" his son. Meanwhile, Dia's kidnappers, have brainwashed Dia and conditioned him to be a ruthless killer. He is even given a new name, "See No More," and is lied to about his family. The RUF has made him commit terrible atrocities to the point where he cannot even remember his former identity or family.

After his escape from slavery, Solomon chases his son across the continent of Africa, risking his life time and again to save his son. There is a powerful scene when this father comes face to face with his son who hardly remembers the life they once shared together. The father looks up to see his son pointing a gun at him.

Solomon Vandy says, "Dia. What are you doing?! Dia!! Look at me. Look at me!! What are you doing?"

Walking towards his son very carefully, he continues, "You are Dia Vandy of the Proumanday Tribe. You are a good boy. You love soccer and school. Your mother loves you so much. She waits by the fire making plantains and red stew. And the new baby…. the cows wait for you, and Bakwu, the wild dog who minds no one but you. Mmm? I know they made you do bad things. You are not a bad boy. I am your father, who loves you. And you will come home with me and be my son…again." Dia lowers the gun and they embrace.

Without the voice of the Father, we can forget who we are. In our "lostness" we often do unspeakable things in this world.

Part of what it means to be a Christ-follower is that we are on a life-long journey of remembering who we were when we lived in Eden with our Father.

In Genesis 27 there is a sad story of how Jacob tricked his blind father, Isaac, into giving him the family blessing instead of the older twin and favored son, Esau. He did it by cooking Isaac's favorite meal, wearing Esau's clothes, and even putting the hide of a goat on his hands, arms, and neck to simulate the hairiness of Esau. It worked. Isaac was fooled and gave the blessing of belovedness to the unintended son, and the family was fragmented beyond repair.

Jacob went to great lengths, took enormous risks in order to get the blessing of belovedness. But what he dared not do was stand before his father as himself. He had to dress up and pretend to be someone else in order to get the blessing. Almost everyone I know is pretending to be someone they aren't in order to find approval and the blessing of the beloved. I have spent years trying to be _____. You can fill in the blank.

I stand before my Father and pray with Augustus Toplady:

> *Nothing in my hand I bring,*
> *Simply to the cross I cling;*
> *Naked, come to Thee for dress;*
> *Helpless look to Thee for grace;*
> *Foul, I to the fountain fly;*
> *Wash me, Savior, or I die.*

It is at the cross that I find the great exchange. Jesus became cursed so that I might be blessed, and when I receive that blessing, I find my way home.

I've discovered that in counting my blessings and claiming them, my own blessedness always leads to a deep desire to bless others. As the "blessed ones" we can walk through this world and offer blessings. It doesn't require much effort. It flows naturally from our hearts, when we listen and count...

One night on the Pacific Crest Trail, a retired police officer from L.A. began telling us cop stories. They were profane, vulgar, and even racist in some ways. At one point I asked him what all of the carnage he witnessed did to his soul. He looked at me blankly. I said, "All of that evil and hatred, pain and suffering—it went somewhere inside you. Where did it go?" Again, a blank look.

Then he asked, "What do you do when you aren't hiking the PCT?"

"I'm a pastor," I said.

He swore, hemmed and hawed a little, and said something about gallows humor and that he felt God protected him. Then he changed the subject.

The next morning he and his son and three other hikers were sitting at a table drinking coffee as I was walking across the parking lot towards the trailhead. I waved at them, trying to catch up with my hiking buddy. Then something told me to go back. I turned around and walked back towards them. They watched me approach—smiling. The cop shouted, "Forget something, Rev?"

"Yes," I said, as I got closer. "I have something I want to give you." I stood before them and raised both hands, palms out towards them and said:

> The Lord bless you and keep you;
> The Lord make His face shine upon you,
> And be gracious to you;
> The Lord lift up His countenance upon you,
> And give you peace.

The cop looked at me slack-jawed and then they all said in unison, "Amen."

Listen to the voice of your Heavenly Father and see if you hear the echo of Eden in these words: "I know that sin has made you do bad things. You are not a bad person. I am your Father, who loves you. And you will come home with me and be my child...again."

The Sacrifice

Then God said, "Take now your son, your only son Isaac,
whom you love, and go to the land of Moriah…"

~ Genesis 22:2

The Pulitzer Prize winning novel by Cormac McCarthy *The Road,* describes the journey south taken by a young boy and his father after an unnamed catastrophe has struck the world. The man and the boy, who also remain unnamed throughout the entire novel, travel through the rough terrain of the southeastern United States.

The conditions they face are unforgiving: rotted corpses, landscapes devastated by fire, abandoned towns and houses. These two travelers are among the few living creatures remaining on earth who have not been driven to murder, rape, and cannibalism.

The father and his son struggle to survive in the harsh weather with little food, supplies, or shelter. Along the way, they must escape from those who might seek to steal from them or, even worse, to kill them for food. Despite their hardships, the man and the child remain determined to survive, reaffirming to themselves that they are the "good guys" who do not seek to harm others.

The father over and over again reminds the boy that they are the ones that are "carrying the fire." The boy in particular retains his unquenchable humanity against all odds, consistently seeking to help the tattered remnants of living humans they encounter.

The relationship can be summed up in a sentence at the beginning of the novel:

"Then they set out along the blacktop in the gunmetal light, shuffling through the ash, each the other's world entire."

Anyone who is a parent knows how true a sentence that is. In this story, God appears to Father Abraham and asks him to give up his world entire; to extinguish the fire of his life.

It is a dark road, this road to Moriah. It's dark because it means Abraham is losing his son, whom he loves. But it's not just that. It's dark because it means losing his dream, for Isaac was the promise of God. Isaac was the promise that Abraham's life would lead to a new community, and he was losing his dream.

Abraham, in this moment, is stepping out into what could be called "the road of god-forsakenness," when it seems like God is contradicting himself, when it seems like God wants to stop the salvation that he's begun.

This is a story about darkness. Most of us, at some point or another in our lives, understand what it is to walk in darkness. Faith is about hanging on in dark places. **Faith is not about doubt-free certainty. Faith is about tenacious obedience at all costs.**

One of my favorite artists is the Dutch master, Rembrandt. I have a print of his version of *The Return of the Prodigal Son* hanging in my study. I love that image. But a close second is the backstory of Rembrandt's rendition of this story in Genesis. A piece entitled *Abraham's Sacrifice.*

Early in his life, he depicted this story in an epic painting. He was a celebrated and prodigiously gifted artist who, in his own personal life was living far from God, but he painted this story for a patron. He used a huge canvas and painted this action moment that is really nothing more than a murder in progress.

There is young and innocent Isaac bare-chested and sprawled out on a rock with old Abraham's left hand pressing the boy's face back, as if to expose his throat, his right hand extended to reach for a knife. All the while an angel has flown up behind him, with panic on his face, and grabs the right hand, knocking the knife from Abraham's grasp.

That's his painting of this story as a young man.

44

But then decades later in life Rembrandt knew what it was like to lose a child in death. He lost several children, in fact. He also came to be convinced of the love of God for him in the person of Jesus of Nazareth, and he began living as a follower of Jesus. Then, as an old man having lost children of his own leaving him with only one son left so late in life—he depicts this scene again.

He does it differently. He does it on an etching plate. And in that version of this scene, Abraham shelters Isaac with his arms around his son, cradling him to his chest, covering the boy's eyes. The expression on Abraham's face is one of sorrow and love. And behind Abraham there is a strong, sheltering angel who cradles this father as the father cradles his son.

This version of the story was done by someone who knew how far God was willing to go to embrace us. Our heavenly Father was willing to lose a Son, so that He might gain people like Rembrandt and me back into his forever family. This is our good news: that God shelters and cradles us even when it seems that we are walking into the unknown darkness where the fire has gone out. And because of Jesus, you and I can say to the Living God, even at our darkest times, "Here I am."

So, may you learn to trust God even in the moments that you don't understand Him. Then and only then will you be *each the other's world entire.*

Friends and Monsters

Love from the ultimate Friend is transformative and insecurities melt away like butter on a warm stove.

A few months ago, I watched the end of the 1935 movie *Bride of Frankenstein*. If you remember the premise of the story, a scientist named Frankenstein created a monster out of the body parts of various cadavers he had scavenged from morgues and graves. Eventually the monster comes to "life" but is so hideous and broken that he frightens the local community and is driven away out into the wilderness where monsters belong. Out in the wild the monster is seen stumbling through the woods, having escaped the castle, and comes upon a blind hermit living alone in a remote section of the forest. With growls and grunts, he looks in the window of the blind hermit's cottage and sees the guy on his knees praying, "Oh, God, please bring me a friend to alleviate my terrible loneliness."

The monster crashes through the door roaring and, of course, the blind guy can't see his hideous face. All the blind hermit knows is the low rumble of the growls of the monster. So unknowingly he says to the monster, "Oh, you must have an affliction; so do I. Perhaps we can be friends."

The hermit starts to love the monster. He feeds him; he speaks kindly to him, makes things for him, and gives him some porridge. The monster doesn't quite know what to do. He has never experienced the love of a friend before. And in this brief three-minute clip the monster smiles for the first time, he speaks for the first time…he starts to humanize.

Some hunters come along and see the monster and they try to kill it. In its panic the monster knocks over a lantern and starts the cottage on fire. People die…and the monster is back out in the dark woods, groping and growling, but every once in a while you recognize the word, "Friend? Friend?"

You know if we could visually depict our self-image, it might look like a Frankenstein monster. We are a cobbled up patchwork of personas received from all kinds of sources: a stitch here from our parents, a stitch there from our friends. Stitches from coaches and teachers and mass media—the icons of our pop culture—get assimilated and we become a hideous expression of what the Creator originally had in mind. We are fragmented and incoherent. As a result, we are lonely and afraid.

What you and I need is a Friend who will come along and with the power of His love, show us that we are loved. And not only that, we are forever safe in that love. We need a Friend whose love will completely overcome all of those distorted images and give us a coherent, human face.

I read somewhere that the 19th century Baptist preacher Charles Spurgeon said that on the cross Jesus, through swollen eyes, looked at the people who beat Him, mocked Him, spit on Him, cursed Him, and abandoned Him, and in the greatest act of friendship in the history of the world—He stayed on the cross.

Why did He do that? To humanize us.

I have called you friends.

~ John 15:15

The Struggle

Then Jacob was left alone; and a Man wrestled with him until the breaking of day.

~ Genesis 32:24

". . . together through ages of the world we have fought the long defeat."

~ Galadriel

Jacob is one of our ancestors in the faith who is in the fight of his life and this is a long defeat that becomes a profound transformational moment.

Jacob stood alone on the northern bank of the river: before him the roaring waters; behind him a wall of Nubian sandstone, perpendicular from its foot to the tangled black forest on its brow; right of him there was nothing except a stony, wet plateau; and left of him, nothing.

Night was descending. The gorge grew gloomier, leaving only a path of sky above him, where stars filled the blackness with such tiny lights that he felt small and solitary.

It had been Jacob's intent to make a private crossing of the Jabbok. But maybe he trusted the swimming stroke of his strong arm better in daylight than in the dark; and maybe the night fell faster within the walls of the gorge than he had expected. Whatever the reason, he did not dive into the waters. He did not move. He stood transfixed, surrounded by sound and soon by an absolute darkness—for even the tiny stars were suddenly swallowed as if by a beast of horrible size.

Jacob felt wind, then chill.

Someone came flying down the riverbank. Jacob felt what he could not see. Then someone attacked him, struck him to the stony ground, and began to wrestle with him. They wrestled by the river. They whirled and heaved each other against the sheer rock wall. In a breathless silence, they wrestled all night until a high grey dawn began to streak the sky.

Jacob's adversary touched the hollow of his thigh and put his thigh out of joint. Jacob threw his arms around a huge waist and held on.

Crippled and bone-tired, in that liminal space between night and day, he sees the face of his adversary. And it is fiercer than the face of death itself—he discovers that he is looking at the face of love.

Darkness is the felt absence of God. This is when you do not see God working in your heart. This is when you are praying and praying and praying…and no answers. This is when you're reading and reading and reading…and getting nothing out of it. It is completely bone dry. These are desert times. These are winter times. This is when God is painfully absent.

Could it be that your frantic struggle for approval; for someone to know you completely and still love you; your life-long wrestle for security; your desperate ache for love—at the bottom of that is an ache for God? Could it be possible that all your life has been leading and preparing you for this moment in the darkness to see the fierce face of Love?

But it is in the wrestling with God that we have the invitation to realize that God is all that we need. If we have Him, we have everything.

God seldom massages me into maturity and transformation.; God wrestles me into spiritual maturity.

This is how it worked with Alexander Solzhenitsyn, a Russian novelist, historian, and short story writer. He was an outspoken critic of the Soviet Union and communism and helped to raise global awareness of its Gulag forced labor camp system.

He was successful and cynical in his prime as a writer until he spoke ill of Josef Stalin privately to a friend who turned him in. He spent the next decades of his life in the Gulag in Siberia.

Listen to his words about his struggle...

It was only when I lay there on rotting prison straw that I sensed within myself the first stirrings of good. Gradually it was disclosed to me that the line separating good and evil passes not through states, nor between classes, nor between political parties either—but right through every human heart—and through all human hearts.... That is why I turn back to the years of my imprisonment and say, sometimes to the astonishment of those about me: **"Bless you, prison!"**.

This is someone whom God wrestled into transformation. His darkness and struggle forced him out of his comfort and caused him to hang on to God for dear life.

Is it possible that in your darkest moments, that the living God is trying to get a hold of you? Is it possible that the living God is graciously nearby? And there, in the dark, he allows you to struggle with Him; to ask your questions, and during those questions, God, with a feather-lite touch, wrestles you into a transformed life.

That is a magnificent defeat.

The Song

Mary stood outside by the tomb weeping.

~ John 20:11

Not too long ago I read an article in *The Atlantic* about the state of Jazz in America, written by a man named David Hadju. He describes the experience of visiting a jazz club. As the band begins to warm up and moves into its first set of songs, he thinks he sees the great jazz trumpeter Wynton Marsalis. Here is how he describes the scene...

> "Excuse me," I whispered to the fellow next to me (a jazz guitarist, I later learned). "Is that Wynton Marsalis?"
>
> "I very seriously doubt that," he snapped back.
>
> The fourth song was a solo showcase for the trumpeter, who, I could now see, was indeed Marsalis, but who no more sounded than looked like what I expected. He played a ballad, "I Don't Stand a Ghost of a Chance With You," unaccompanied. Written by Victor Young, a film-score composer, for a 1930s romance, the piece can bring out the sadness in any scene, and Marsalis appeared deeply attuned to its melancholy. He performed the song in murmurs and sighs, at points nearly talking the words in notes. It was a wrenching act of creative expression.
>
> When he reached the climax, Marsalis played the final phrase, the title statement, in declarative tones, allowing each successive note to linger in the air a bit longer. "I don't stand... a ghost ... of ... a ... chance..." The room was silent until, at the most dramatic point,

someone's cell phone went off, blaring a rapid singsong melody in electronic bleeps. People started giggling and picking up their drinks. The moment—the whole performance—unraveled.

Marsalis paused for a beat, motionless, and his eyebrows arched. I scrawled on a sheet of notepaper, MAGIC, RUINED.

I tell you this story because, in many ways, it describes Mary's life. The magic of her life was ruined when Jesus died on the cross.

Her hope was Jesus. He had changed her life, and she had followed him ever since. He had cast seven demons out of her freeing her from untold torment. He had given her life...a reason to live...a place in the kingdom. He had given her worth and dignity...understanding... compassion...love... And he had given her hope.

Now that hope lay at the bottom of her heart, flat and lifeless.

But something helps her survive that cruel moment. Something resilient, like a blade of grass that springs up after being stepped on. That something is love.

Love brought Mary to his cross. And love brings her now to his grave.

The early church looked at Mary, weary with weeping grief just outside the tomb of Jesus, as a symbol of the whole world. Mary's tears are the tears of Fresno where a man gunned down three random men in an apparent hate crime. Mary's tears are the tears of Colombo, Sri Lanka when a garbage dump collapsed and crashed into nearby homes, killing dozens.

Mary's tears are the tears of the family of Robert Godwin Sr., 74, a former foundry worker and father of 10, who was picking up aluminum cans on Sunday when he was shot and the video of it was posted on social media. Mary's tears are the tears of the families of those killed by poisonous gas attacks in Syria that killed at least 86 people, including 26 children.

Mary's tears are the tears of your life, too. Mary is a stand-in for all the grief and suffering of the world. But here is what is important to remember: It is to Mary in the predawn dark, in her most painful moment, that Jesus appears.

Of all the people that Jesus could have revealed himself to, he chooses Mary first.

Peter and John had been there earlier in the morning, but they didn't see angels. Angels only turn up for Mary and her tears. Maybe it's because, sometimes, you can only see angels through tears.

Easter is not about escaping this sorry dark world into the next world. Easter is about tearing a hole in the fabric that separates this world from the next so that heaven can get into this world.

My son Clinton and I share a favorite artist, Jack Johnson. He has a song that describes the complexities of life in the 21st century. It is a song filled with pain, sorrow and the angst of our times. But he has a line that serves as a refrain that says:

> *There were so many fewer questions*
> *When stars were still just the holes to heaven.*

I love that imagery. Next time you step outside and look up to see the stars, think of them as tiny holes in the floor of heaven.

Easter is a Grand Canyon size hole in the floor of heaven. The eternal came flooding into our world through that opening when the stone was rolled away. The bodily resurrection of Jesus is a foretaste of the renewal, re-integration and restoration that is coming when the 'thy-will-be-done-on-earth-as-it-is-in-heaven' part of our Lord's prayer is answered once and for all.

Here's the point of Easter: **God loves this world.**

Sometimes I've said to skeptics that don't yet believe in our faith that they should at least hope our faith is true; because it makes so much sense of the longings that are latent in all of our souls.

I love what Tolkien says,

> We all long for [Eden], and we are constantly glimpsing it: our whole nature...is still soaked with the sense of 'exile'.

You, your children, and grandchildren may have walked away from the Church, but deep down they long for what the church stands for to be true. They have an ache for Eden.

The thirst for spirituality is not an illusion. It is there because we were made for another reality—God. Because God is our home. Your deep passion for health, education for children, justice in the world, and beauty in your life—these things are not random desires. They are within us because they are a part of a world created by a God who made it to operate that way.

Why did my oldest son, Cole, take his four children to a park in Tacoma yesterday to pick up trash and celebrate Earth Day? Because he is a New Age, liberal, tree-hugger? No, because for my son, who loves Jesus as passionately as any man I know, how we respect this earth is a reflection of our love for the Creator-God who created the first garden called paradise and came back to life in a second garden of tombs.

David Hadju sat stunned in the back of the jazz club as the magic that he experienced in the room was ruined. But I want you to listen to what happened next...

> The cell-phone offender scooted into the hall as the chatter in the room grew louder. Still frozen at the microphone, Marsalis replayed the silly cell-phone melody note for note. Then he repeated it, and began improvising variations on the tune. The audience slowly came back to him. In a few minutes he resolved the improvisation—which had changed keys once or twice and throttled down to a ballad tempo—and ended up exactly where he had left off: "I... don't... stand... a... ghost... of... a...chance... with... you..." The ovation was tremendous.

That is a small picture of what God has done for us, and the world, at the empty tomb of Jesus. All the ways that we are unraveled, all the ways that we are ruined—Jesus uses all of that and transforms them into a restoration and healing.

Jesus has taken our brokenness, tears, and ruin—and he has refashioned it into a redemption song.

Till He Comes

For as often as you eat this bread and drink this cup,
you proclaim the Lord's death till He comes.

~ 1 Corinthians 11:26

What will Jesus bring with Him when He returns? Some believe He will bring wrath, death and judgment. One popular talk radio host says that we are living in Biblical times and, in the not too distant future, things are going to be so bad that people in our country will resort to cannibalism. He bases this belief, not on the Bible, but on the Book of Mormon.

I am not a Latter Day Saint, but I will concede that when Jesus returns to this earth He will bring a meal with Him. It will be a wonderful, sumptuous meal that will satisfy every human longing. (Rev. 19:7-9; 21:1-5a)

When we get to the new heavens and the new earth, it will be a Supper! There will be no more pain and suffering, crying, death, or sorrow. No hunger, longings, or emptiness; they will all be gone. In their place will be joy unspeakable and full of glory. There will be delight, dancing, full-throated laughter, and full stomachs. There will be complete and utter satisfaction.

So, what are the Communion elements, the bread and the cup? These are the appetizers of your future bliss.

When you take Communion, God is whispering in your ear, "Feel the texture of this bread; it's the body of my son. Taste the tang of this cup on your lips; it's the blood of my Son. I am unconditionally committed to getting you home. There is nothing more I can say. There is nothing more I can do."

In the book *The Lord of the Rings,* there is a siege of the great city Minas Tirith. One of the hobbits, named Pippin, is scared. He hears the battle drums of the orcs and trolls. He feels the vibrations of the siege machines rolling towards the walls. He is convinced that he is going to die along with everyone in the city. The evil hordes begin to beat on the gates, scale the walls, and invade the city. And just when all seems lost, he hears a distant horn. The blast of the battle horn of Rohan resounds in the valley, signaling a massive army of men to attack the flank of the besieging army of orcs. The battle lines are broken and Pippin, the city, and everyone in it is saved.

Tolkien then tells us that for the rest of his life, Pippin could never hear a distant horn without breaking into tears. The sound of the horn was an audible reminder of his salvation and the time he heard it. He relived his salvation and it connected him to his past. He remembered the sacrifice of the people who died to save him. No matter what kind of foul mood Pippin might be in, he couldn't stay grumpy. When he heard the horn, it reminded him that every single moment of the rest of his life was a gift of grace.

Take, eat, and listen.

Lions or Dragons

Then the [dragon] said to the woman, "You will not surely die. For God knows that in the day you eat of it your eyes will be opened, and you will be like God"

~ Genesis 3:4-5

Traditionally, sin is thought to refer to the "bad things people do", such as stealing, adultery, gossiping, judging, and the like. William Temple pointed out that these things are merely symptoms of a deeper problem. He says there is only one Sin: putting ourselves in the center of our lives and other people's lives where only God should be. Sins with a small "s" are those specific things we do as a result of placing ourselves in the center of our world.

We play God by denying our humanity and trying to control everything for selfish reasons. I've noticed that when my world gets out of control, I often try to control the myriad of little things over which I have power. The more insecure I am, the more I am driven to control. We try our best to control people. Parents try to control kids; kids try to control parents. Wives try to control husbands; husbands try to control wives. Coworkers vie for office control. Everyone has his preferred methods: Guilt and shame, praise and affirmation, anger, fear, or an old favorite—the silent treatment.

We attempt to control our problems, thinking, "I can handle it. It's not really a problem. I'm fine." We become experts at pain-management. How much time and effort do you spend running from pain? Avoiding it, denying it, escaping it, reducing it, or postponing it? We avoid it by: Eating, not eating, drinking, smoking, shopping, abusing prescription drugs, exercise, traveling, or serial relationships. Others withdraw into

58

a hole, building a protective wall of depression around them.

The real pain comes when we realize that no matter how hard we try, we're not in control. That insight can be very scary. In our culture we have come to believe that any pain in our lives is a violation of our spiritual rights. But the truth about pain may be very different. As Keith Miller has said, "Freedom comes when the acid of your pain eats through the wall of your denial."

C.S. Lewis pictures our struggle in facing the reality of who we are in his children's book *Voyage of the Dawn Treader*. The lion Aslan, the Christ-figure, confronts a very unkind, mean, and stubborn little boy named Eustace Scrubb. His transformation into a dragon is a picture of what happens when we seek to be God and live for our own power and glory. This "leads to the most bestial and cruel kind of behavior." Likewise, Eustace's restoration or renewal represents the transformation of the gospel of Jesus Christ.

Eustace clearly lusted for power, expressing it in the mean and petty ways that only a schoolboy could: teasing, torturing animals, tattling, and ingratiating himself to adult authorities. When Eustace found the dragon's treasure he was elated and imagined the life of ease and power he would now have. When he woke, however, to his horror, he had turned into a hideous dragon. His transformation into a dragon was a natural consequence of his obsession. Because he thought like a dragon, he had become a dragon. When we set our hearts on power, we become hardened predators. We become like what we worship.

The shock of his transformation humbled Eustace and he longed to be a normal boy again. As his pride faded, the idolatry in his heart began to be healed. One night Eustace the dragon met a mysterious lion. The lion challenged him to "undress," to take off his dragon skin. Eustace managed to peel off a layer, but found he was still a dragon underneath. He tried repeatedly, but made no further progress.

Eustace relates to character Edmond:

> The lion finally said, 'You will have to let me undress you.' I was afraid of his claws, I can tell you, but I was pretty nearly desperate now. So I just lay flat on my back to let him do it. The very first tear he made was so deep that I thought it had gone right into my heart. And when he began pulling the skin off, it hurt worse than anything I've ever felt [...] Well, he peeled the beastly stuff right off – just as I thought I'd done it myself the other three times, only they hadn't hurt – and there it was lying on the grass: only ever so much thicker, and darker, and more knobbly-looking than the others had been. And there was I, as smooth and soft as a peeled switch and smaller than I had been [...] I'd turned into a boy again.
>
> 'After a bit the lion took me out and dressed me.'
>
> 'Dressed you? With his paws?'
>
> 'Well, I don't exactly remember that bit. But he did somehow or other: in new clothes—the same I've got on now, as a matter of fact. And then suddenly I was back here. Which is what makes me think it must have been a dream.'
>
> 'No. It wasn't a dream,' said Edmund.
>
> 'Why not?'
>
> 'Well, there are clothes, for one thing. And you have been—well, un-dragoned, for another.'
>
> 'What do you think it was, then?' asked Eustace.
>
> 'I think you've seen Aslan,' said Edmund.

Eustace's experience here vividly illustrates that the cure for playing God is to admit you are utterly powerless.

When I believe that truth down deep in my life, down where the knobs are, then I find peace and hope.

I become "un-dragoned." And so can you.

A Distant Shadow

Sometimes you hear a television reporter interview a celebrity asking if he has any regrets in his life. I am always astounded that, without hesitation, most celebrities say no. If they had to do it all over again, they would live their lives the same way. How can that be? Have they never made any mistakes?

I talk to plenty of folks that assure me everyone who lives in the real world has regrets. The question is: how do we live with them? Some pretend they don't have any. I imagine this is the way of shallow celebrities or professional athletes. They allow that any miniscule mistake really only contributed to the larger mosaic and milieu that made them the artist they are.

Another strategy is to let our regrets define our identity. You see this sometimes in those in recovery. "Hi, I'm Joe. I'm a regretter."

"Hi, Joe. Welcome to our meeting and thanks for sharing, Joe. Cookies and Kool-Aid will be served after tonight's meeting."

There is no daylight between who they are and what they have done that deserves their regret and remorse. It is a permanent scar that disfigures their soul. Their regrets are a calling card to gain them some street cred to talk to and ostensibly help other regretters. It takes a regretter to reach a regretter is their mantra.

Might there be a third way — to live with regrets as a contributing part of your life without marking your identity in such a way that others are not put off by your scarlet wounds?

The film *A Beautiful Mind* tells the story of John Nash, a brilliant mathematician whose career and life were crippled by schizophrenia. Nash taught at MIT until delusions took over his

61

life. After years of struggle, he began teaching at Princeton and went on to win the Nobel Prize for his theory of the dynamics of human conflict as it relates to economics. Three characters support Nash in his life struggles: a roommate from Princeton, a little girl who is his niece whom he adores, and William Parchment, a top-secret government operative. All three characters are integral to Nash's view of reality. The only problem is that they are delusions. They certainly seem real to John Nash whose greatest strength, the beautiful mind, lets him down.

Toward the end of the movie Nash is invited into the professors' lounge by a man who has just told him he's being considered for the Nobel Prize. Nash is uncertain of how he should respond; he wonders if his mind is fabricating a dream. He even asks a student whether the man is real or a hallucination. When Nash is convinced that the man and his invitation are genuine, he still resists, feeling unworthy of the exclusivity of the professors' lounge. He is reluctant to enter the lounge, aware that his episodes of psychotic behavior are well known by faculty. As the messenger from the Nobel Prize committee strolls with Nash to the faculty lounge, they engage in an awkward conversation as to the stability of Nash's mental state:

> "The awards are substantial. They require private funding. As such, the image of the Nobel is..."
>
> "I see. You came here to find out if I was crazy? Find out if I would...screw everything up if I actually won? Dance around the podium, strip naked, and squawk like a chicken, things of this nature?"
>
> "Something like that, yes."
>
> "Would I embarrass you? Yes, it is possible. You see, I...I am crazy. I take the newer medications, but I still see things that are not here. I just choose not to acknowledge them. Like a diet of the mind, I choose not to indulge certain appetites. Like my appetite for patterns."

As they have this conversation, the three characters—Charles, the niece, and William Parchment—all walk in pace with Nash and the messenger from the Nobel Prize committee, but off to the side like distant shadows. He glances at them, but he doesn't engage them. They are a part of who he is, but he is defined by something that transcends those ever-present delusions.

That's what I choose to do with my scarlet regrets. They are always with me, but I choose not to indulge in the appetite of self-pity. I choose not to be identified by my regrets. I choose, instead, to live in the light of a transcendent reality: I am a favored son of the Most High God. I am an heir and joint heir with Jesus Christ.

Nash walks warily through the gothic entrance and sits at a table. Unexpectedly, the professors begin to walk over to John's table and lay down their pens in front of him. This is a tradition Princeton faculty use to honor highly esteemed colleagues. One by one, the professors acknowledge their love and support for the troubled man who, despite difficulties, stayed the course: "It's an honor, John." "It's a privilege, John." "Congratulations, John."

One day I will be allowed entrance into a great hall and sit at a table and the King will say, "To him who overcomes I will give him [...] a white stone, and on the stone a new name written which no one knows except him who receives it" (*New King James Version,* Rev. 2:17).

So long, regrets.

Wait, the King is Coming

A voice of one calling:
"In the wilderness prepare
the way for the LORD;
make straight in the desert
a highway for our God.
Every valley shall be raised up,
every mountain and hill made low;
the rough ground shall become level,
the rugged places a plain.
And the glory of the LORD will be revealed,
and all people will see it together.
For the mouth of the LORD has spoken."

~ Isaiah 40: 3-5

The hearer of these words in ancient times would have recognized this as an announcement of a coming king. Back then when the king came to your community, you built him a new road. Building highways and boulevards was symbolic of what kingship is all about. Knocking down barriers and bridging gaps got rid of all resistance to the physical presence of the king. Likewise, we are to remove any personal resistance we might have towards the king. We are not supposed to hold anything back.

Authority, rightfully exercised, is like rain falling on parched ground to those under that authority. Flourishing abounds. These verses tell us when the King comes to the impassable wilderness it will become passable. When the King comes, the desolate and uninhabitable wilderness becomes habitable. The coming King will display His authority and bring healing to the land. However, this is no ordinary king. When human kings come, you build a bridge over the ravine; when this King comes, the ravine vanishes. When human kings come, a better pass might be constructed through the mountains; when this King comes, the mountains are brought down.

Isaiah draws on one of the deepest and most enduring hopes of the human race. The whole planet is desolate and like an uninhabitable wilderness. Death, disease, war, poverty, strife, abuse, and brokenness are commonplace, and yet, a King is coming that can put things to rights.

In the movie *Lord of the Rings, Return of the King,* there is a scene in which the steward of Gondor, who has occupied the throne for generations, has gone mad. With his two sons dead at the hands of the army of Mordor, he decides to commit suicide in the funeral pyre for his son Faramir. At the same time the heir to the throne of Gondor approaches with a liberating army. The usurper is leaving the throne and the rightful heir is returning. It is a very low moment: darkness all around, storms of war rumbling, and hope is all but lost. But then the dead tree of Gondor sprouts one small white flower in recognition of the return of Aragorn, the king, to the city.

The best and deepest stories understand there is an ache for a king that will put things to rights and bring healing to the land because it suffers under incompetent managers or stewards. And when the ultimate King comes, He will bring healing. As Isaiah says in verse 5, "All mankind together will see it."

This is the King of the whole world. He comes from outside the world. Isaiah says a true King is coming who has absolute authority and brings absolute healing. Isaiah says, "Wait, He is coming!"

> But those who wait on the LORD
> Shall renew their strength;
> They shall mount up with wings like eagles,
> They shall run and not be weary,
> They shall walk and not faint.
>
> (*New King James Version*, Is. 40:31)

To wait means to obey. You are not treating Him as King unless you are willing to say, "not my will but Thine be done," in every ravine and mountain of life.

To wait means to relax. "God, your schedule, not mine. I accept the fact that I don't know what's best. I humble myself beneath you." Worry is always a resistance to the Kingship of Jesus. Worry always means if I were in charge, I would do a better job.

To wait means to expect, to hope. Wait means if the Lordship of Jesus is a healing influence, then I am not treating God as King unless I have high expectations of what He can do through me. Some do not treat God as the Great King because all they can see are the great problems in their world: Problems in politics, in the family, at work, at church; Problems in the economy, problems in life. We sigh and say, "That is just the way things are going to be."

When you have that outlook, you reveal that you are not treating Him as King.

> *Thou art coming to a King,*
> *Large petitions with thee bring;*
> *For His grace and power are such,*
> *None can ever ask too much;*
> *None can ever ask too much.*

> ~ John Newton

To the degree you relinquish the sphere of your world under His Kingship, there is healing. While these last verses of Isaiah 40 have been special to me for years for their poetic beauty, it wasn't until recently that I finally had an answer to a question that has bugged me. Logically, the order should be as follows:

1. I will walk and not faint,

2. I will run and not grow weary,

3. I will soar on wings like eagles.

66

But that is not the order in Isaiah. The correct order is: Soar . . . Run . . . Walk. Walking is the point. Sometimes you will soar, but you won't always soar. You will always be able to walk, when Jesus is your King.

Why We Worship Jesus

What would you nominate as the number one priority of the church? Discipleship? Evangelism? Social Justice? Love all mankind? If you said any of those you would be wrong. In Matt. 22:37-38 Jesus said, "You shall love the Lord your God with all your heart, with all your soul, and with all your mind. This is the first and great commandment" (*New King James Version*). Notice that Jesus said loving God is the first and greatest commandment. This speaks to the first order of things and preeminence. It is priority one.

The Westminster Shorter Catechism reads: "What is the chief end of man? To love God and enjoy Him forever." If we get the loving God part wrong, we will be improperly motivated to do the rest. Our evangelism becomes a way to measure our success. Our discipleship becomes a way to puff up our own knowledge. Our activism in social justice will be ego-gratifying, false altruism. Our love will be truncated and stunted because it will have a finite source...us. It is really about Jesus. We have to get this right. All that follows depends on the right beginning.

In Revelation 5 we get a gauzy glimpse of heavenly worship happening right now. The apostle John is in prison in a penal colony on the isle of Patmos. He tells us what he sees in heaven. The elders, angels, and a host of heavenly creatures are singing loud songs of praise about the Lamb—Jesus: "And they sang a new song, saying: 'You are worthy to take the scroll, and to open its seals; for You were slain'" (Verse 9). He took our punishment. In Gethsemane Jesus prayed, "Father, if you are willing, take this cup from me; yet not my will, but yours be done" (*New International Version,* Luke 22:42). Jesus wasn't horrified by the prospect of physical suffering. Others had faced worse physical pain than Jesus. That's not why He sweat blood and recoiled in horror at the cross. It was the fact that He was to become at His core…sin. He became the personification, the embodiment, and the expression of vile depravity.

Think of your worst sin. Now remember when the Holy Spirit convicted you and you saw, with blinding clarity, the ugliness of that particular sin. Remember how you felt? The shame. The guilt. Now multiply that feeling by the thousands of experiences of sin in your life. Multiply that feeling again by the billions and billions of people who have ever lived. War, murder, sexual abuse, deceit, gossip, greed, racism—Imagine now, one person experiencing within Himself the indescribable nightmare of that guilt and remorse…as if He had done each thing—bearing the weight of all that. And imagine that one person not just feeling separated from God, as horrible as that is; imagine that person being the focus of God's wrath. That was the cup Jesus begged to be spared, the cup of God's wrath towards the sins of God's people whom He loves. Imagine that burden falling on a heart that from eternity past had never known the slightest shadow of guilt. Imagine that wrath falling on a heart that had never known a split second of separation from God.

My friends, you will never face the wrath of God for your sins. All you will ever know is the smile of God on your life. All you will ever know for all eternity is God's grace. That's why the angels and the elders sing this new song. Because Jesus took our wrath and set us free. "And they sang a new song, saying: 'You are worthy […] for You […] have redeemed us to God by Your blood,'" (*New King James Version,* Rev. 5:9). He purchased us with His blood. "For even the Son of Man [came to]… give His life a ransom for many" (Mark 10:45).

In Jesus's day when someone became a slave, his or her freedom was set at a price. Yet he or she could earn a modicum of a wage so that, in theory, he or she could purchase his or her freedom. That rarely happened. Someone else might pay the ransom, but even that didn't happen very often. Slaves typically lived all their lives knowing that freedom was just a ransom's price away, yet knowing they would never be able to pay it. They would die slaves. Can you imagine living with that just out of reach?

In the movie *Schindler's List* we see a modern picture of this. It is the story of a wealthy man named Oscar Schindler who sees a whole race of people headed for destruction. He realizes he could use his factories and wealth to buy human lives and save them from death. In one scene he's moved a group of people to his factory, but their children and their wives are on a train headed for destruction. He approaches the Nazi officer and pours out a little bag of diamonds, saying, "I want to buy those people." When the war is over and the death camps are finally liberated, he is surrounded by hundreds of lives that he saved. He thinks of all the lives not saved. He breaks down and begins to weep, saying, "I could have done more. I could have done more. I could have sold this car." He takes off his watch and says, "How many would this have purchased? I could have sold this to buy more. I could have given up more to save them."

That picture is a small glimpse of the heart of God, Who says, "I would give everything I have to buy every life I can." As Paul wrote, "You were bought at a price" (*New International Version,* 1 Cor. 6:20).

Why do we worship Jesus? Because "He was wounded for our transgressions, He was bruised for our iniquities; the chastisement for our peace was upon Him, and by His stripes we are healed" (*New King James Version,* Is. 53:5).

I don't know about you, but I love Him. I worship Jesus because He took my punishment and because He purchased my salvation with His broken body and shed blood. His sacrifice makes me want to join:

> the voice of many angels around the throne, the living creatures, and the elders; and the number of them was ten thousand times ten thousand, and thousands of thousands, saying with a loud voice:

70

'Worthy is the Lamb who was slain
To receive power and riches and wisdom,
And strength and honor and glory and blessing!'
(Rev. 5:11-12)

Changed by a Story

The two ladies seated behind us in the theater were obnoxious. One kept inadvertently kicking the back of my seat. Both were loud talkers. My wife and I heard about almost all of their issues, from a dog that kept pooping in the house to what they bought their kids for Christmas. There was no volume control at all, no matter the topic. One said to the other, "I told Margret I was going to go see *Les Miserables* and she wrinkled her nose up at me and told me that musicals suck." The other lady said, "Of course we are going to see it! Some people don't have any freaking culture." Put that last sentence on a T-shirt and you'll have a bestseller.

They guffawed at each comedic movie trailer, gave a running commentary on whether they would see it or not, shifted in their seats, and continued to kick the back of my chair. My frustration mounted. We had driven to the town north of our city to see this much-anticipated film. All theaters in our city were sold out. Soon the place filled up and no other seats were available. We were stuck right where we were. My wife kept tapping my leg to calm me down.

As the film played out before us with each quiet and pensive moment, my chair was nudged or some comment could be heard about the performance from the ladies behind me. I was not just irritated, I was miserable. And no matter how loud the film score or moving the actors' performance, I could not get past the seeming disregard of personal space from the ladies behind me. It was as if we were in their living room watching a private screening just for them.

I began to anticipate the next boisterous laugh, ill-timed comment, or kick of my seat. I found that, far from immersing myself in this story of grace, I was imagining ways to torture the movie gremlins seated behind me. I could hear them crunching their salty, buttery popcorn, slurping their sodas, and sliding straws through the lids of their super-sized drinks.

I turned my head and looked at them and shot them my best stink-eye, a look that has wilted and withered grown men. Alas, they were engrossed in the film and my evil eye was lost in the dark. I contemplated what I should do: Say something to them? Block them from my mind? How could my wife not notice these demon movie monsters just inches from her ears; was she deaf?

In the midst of this boiling cauldron of irritation, Anne Hathaway, who played the role of Fantine, began to sing:

> *There was a time when men were kind*
> *When their voices were soft*
> *And their words inviting*
> *There was a time when love was blind*
> *And the world was a song*
> *And the song was exciting*
> *There was a time*
> *Then it all went wrong*

Suddenly, the demons were gone. No more kicks to the back of my chair. No more crass comments, nor ill-timed laughter, were heard. I was no longer in the theater. I was transported to Paris and Fantine was singing to me. Then Jean Valjean was giving voice to my longing for love. Then he was praying my prayers for my sons and I was caught up in the story of the triumph of mercy over law and pharisaism. I marveled at beauty juxtaposed with degradation, filled with wonder and the triumph of grace.

When my wife is moved with either fear or other deep emotions during a movie, she gradually tightens her grip on my arm. Sometimes it hurts. When Jean Valjean sang his final prayer for his daughter and her fiancé, my arm was gripped most tightly when the lyrics "To love another person is to see the face of God" were sung. The story of love and grace eclipses all things.

And I wept.

> *What have I done, sweet Jesus, what have I done?*
> *Become a thief in the night, become a dog on the run?*
> *...Is there another way to go?*

Yes, the ladies were still behind me, but I was no longer there. I was immersed in a story of redemption. I'm not sure I went willingly to this place of forgetfulness, but I went nonetheless. I think it would be good for me to go there more often. And if the Gospel is what it claims to be, I don't have to pay for a movie ticket and drive to Marysville to discover that the gremlins of my world disappear in the light of His glory and grace.

Part Three:

Notes from Relationships

While I know myself as a creation of God, I am also obligated to realize and remember that everyone else and everything else are also God's creation.

~ Maya Angelou

It's not what you look at that matters, it's what you see.

~ Henry David Thoreau

You have never talked to a mere mortal.

~ C.S. Lewis

The Bride

Come, I will show you the Bride, the wife of the Lamb.

~ Revelation 21:9

The church gets kicked around a lot these days. Certainly, by those who do not follow Jesus that even makes sense. Why would they be warm to an institution that is antithetical to their way of living? But what hurts my heart is that there are many stone-throwers who attend church and say that they love Jesus. Or they used to attend church and often are the most prolific rock-chuckers.

Often, they sit at home and watch their favorite preacher on T.V. (I'm not going to say much about this approach except to say: It is about as lazy as it gets) However, many are involved in para-church organizations which have taken the place of the church for lots of Christian leaders. Recovery groups, retreat centers, discipleship ministries, itinerant conferences, and denominational gatherings have become the preferred alternative to weekly and often mundane attendance full of sinners led by the chief of sinners—the preacher.

> "Every congregation is a congregation of sinners. As if that weren't bad enough, they all have sinners for pastors" (Eugene Peterson).

Then there are the elite followers of Jesus who decide that it is better to find a small gathering of like-minded believers who really "get it" and know how to live the Christian life on a more authentic, missional, and intentional way. They even take some pride in saying, "I don't go to church, but I love Jesus.

I have two problems with these neo-gnostic approaches to being a Christian. First, I don't see a good example in the Bible of retreating from the messy living and loving of one another outside of the Body of Christ.

Where does one go to devote oneself to "the apostles' teaching and fellowship, to the breaking of bread and prayers" (*New International Version,* Acts 2:42)? Do these ministries administer the sacraments? Do they perform marriages? Do they officiate funerals? Do they take casseroles to the bereaved? Do they visit the hospitals and minister in the nursing homes? Do they go to the jails and listen, love, and pray for broken humanity?

I reckon there are some that do, and I would say they are the exception that proves the rule.

The Biblical testimony and the witness of Christian history is that the Church is the last best hope for this dark world. The bride of Jesus; the body of Christ—these do not describe Young Life, Southern Baptist, or John Eldredge's ministry. They describe the First Methobapterian church in your town.

These ministries are important, and even essential, to the edification of the Church but make no mistake, they are NOT the Church.

But another reason I have a problem with kicking the church to the curb is more personal. I wrote in my journal one morning,

I've been saved twice:
Once in 1965 by Jesus
Again in 1999 by His Bride

In the fall of 1999, I resigned my Church in Colorado and moved my young family to the Pacific Northwest. I had made sinful choices that led to this upheaval. Our destination was a little church in Sumner, Washington. My brother was the pastor of the church, and they welcomed us with open arms in spite of my scarlet reputation.

They had a building fund they used to move us out to Sumner and provide funds for me to go to New Life Clinic in Los

Angeles for a therapy intensive that lasted three weeks.

We were unemployed and homeless. The little church provided us a place to live next door in a house they had purchased and remodeled for Sunday School classes. They gave me a job of tearing down a condemned house next door to that house so that the lot could be used for parking. They paid for Lynette and me to go to marriage counseling sometimes twice a week for over a year. They helped pay the tuition for my oldest son to attend a private Christian school.

More importantly they loved us deeply; they loved us well. They didn't smother us. They weren't cloyingly sweet with their affection. Do you know what they did? They made space for us. It was like they were eating a lavish and wonderful meal at a long table and we were unexpected guests. They scrunched together, got more plates and silverware, and made room for us at their table. That simple act began our healing.

After about a year, they asked me to teach a Sunday School class. Not long after that, my brother had to be out of town, and he asked me to preach for him. It had been about a year and a half since I had preached. I remember standing in front of this little congregation, with tears streaking down my face, saying thank you to them for the honor of preaching to them. A man from the back of the church shouted, "We love you, Joe!"

To shorten this story, in about 3 years that church disbanded. They had exhausted themselves in giving to my family and had run out of everything to stay alive except love. Do you remember that hymn that was sung in the first church found in Philippians chapter two?

> Let the same mind be in you that was in Christ Jesus, who, though he was in the form of God, did not regard equality with God as something to be exploited, but **emptied himself...**

If ever there was a church that followed Jesus down into obscurity in the world's eyes and greatness in God's, it was

Christ Church of Sumner.

They gave themselves away, so that my family could stay together and find healing and restoration. Because of their kenosis and agape love, my oldest son met his future wife in that little church and we have four wonderful grandchildren; my other two sons grew up in that little church and made lasting friends. My wife and I just celebrated our thirty-eighth year of marriage. God has graciously allowed me to pastor again, and has given my wife and I ministry to pastors and their families.

All that is to say that I don't take it well when Christians neglect, throw rocks, and bad-mouth the bride of Jesus.

> "There's nobody who doesn't have problems with the church, because there's sin in the church. But there's no other place to be a Christian..." (Eugene Peterson).

So, let me say this as loving as I can. Stop chunking rocks at my Lord's bride or I'll fight you in the church parking lot.

Extra Grace Required

Everyone has a family member that is hard to love. If you don't know who that particularly challenging-to-love person is, chances are it is you. It is quite sobering to imagine that I am someone's hard to love person. In our family that person was my maternal grandfather.

He was a grumpy old cowboy from west Texas. He only had an 8th grade education and, for a few years when my mother was a little girl, he was a Baptist preacher. Then he decided that making money was more important than winning souls, so he went back to combining wheat up and down the Midwest from Texas to Canada.

He was an old man when I was born and much older than his years. His teeth were worn down to the gums on both sides of his mouth from clamping down on a pipe stem for so many years. He never brushed his teeth and only took a bath once a week. To this day there are three smells that make my head spin: Vitalis hair tonic, Prince Albert tobacco smoke, and BENGAY. And that's all I want to say about that.

He was a complicated man and a walking contradiction, my grandfather. He would give the shirt off his back to a complete stranger but was hesitant to buy new clothes for his own children. As family stories go, I've told this one so many times. And it happened so long ago that I can't remember if it happened to me, or to my brother, or to both of us.

One day I was riding with him in his old 1959 blue 3/4-ton Chevrolet pickup up a rough old mountain road in northern New Mexico. He cleared his throat, took the pipe out of his mouth, and began to sing an old hymn:

What a friend we have in Jesus,
All our sins and griefs to bear!
What a privilege to carry
Everything to God in prayer!

About this time in the hymn, suddenly and without warning, we hit a huge pothole in the road that bounced us so hard we both hit our heads on the roof of the cab of the pickup. That's when my grandfather yelled, "God damn these roads!"

Then he went back to singing...

Have we trials and temptations?
Is there trouble anywhere?
We should never be discouraged—
Take it to the Lord in prayer.

I was stunned. I never understood, at such a formative stage in my life, how two disparate things could come out of the same mouth—curses and praises. He was as deeply flawed a man as I have ever known. But you know what? He loved Jesus and he loved me, and that meant I loved him too.

There are people in every family that are hard to love. And what is true of our personal family is true of the family of God. How do we love the hard to love, old, curmudgeonly Christians in the family of God? And how do I love someone who is morally broken?

One day a group of people came to Jesus dragging a disheveled woman who had been caught in adultery. They threw her at his feet. Each held a stone, for the punishment of such a crime was death by stoning. Interestingly, they only brought the woman. This leads me to believe the woman had been framed.

In John Chapter 8, they said, *Teacher, [. . .] What shall we do with her?* (vs 4-5) They didn't care about this woman. She was just a pawn in their game to try to trap Jesus. They knew the Law. They had a lot of truth, but not much grace. Sometimes stones feel good in our hands. They fit like a well-worn tool. Do you ever have a stone in your hand: a judgmental attitude or self-righteous thoughts?

Why do churches produce so many stone throwers? They don't dance. They don't laugh. They don't have much capacity for joy. But there is one thing they do enjoy—passing judgment on other people they regard as spiritually inferior. Someone's kids get a little wild; they pick up a stone. Somebody's marriage isn't working; they pick up a stone. The worship leader chooses the wrong kind of song; they pick up a stone. The pastor posts something on social media they don't like, they pick up a stone. Somebody crosses the line, somebody violates the code, somebody has a problem—word spreads and people start picking up stones.

The truth is that gathering stones energizes them in a way. They almost look forward to it. It kind of makes them feel good. I know what that feels like. Maybe you do too. But the only people attracted to a club of stone-throwers are other stone-throwers. And God forbid you mess up, because you don't want to be around when the rocks start flying.

So Jesus said to all the people who had gathered around Him, Let the one who is without sin cast the first stone. And they all walked away. Then He turned to the woman and said, 'Does no one here condemn you? . . . Then neither do I' (vs. 7,10-11). That's grace—no condemnation from Jesus. But then, He said one more thing to her. He said to her, Now, go and sin no more (v. 11). That's truth.

Preaching to an African American church is very different from preaching in my church because they give you feedback the whole time. If you're doing well, they give you grace. They say, "Preach it! Keep going! Tell it!" If it's not going very well, they give you truth by yelling, "Help him, Jesus!"

What a great thing it would be if, as a Christian community, we could flood folks with grace and truth. When people are doing well, we'd let them know and cheer them on, "Go on! Tell it! Do it!" And when someone messes up, we'd say, "Help 'em, Jesus! Help 'em!"

We are all walking contradictions and God knew just what

we needed. The Apostle John wrote in John 1:14, "And the Word became flesh and dwelt among us, and we beheld His glory, the glory as of the only begotten of the Father, full of grace and truth" (*New King James Version*). There will always be holes in the road of life that bring out the worst in us. We need grace and truth from the family of faith. But when we can't find it there or their hands hold only stones, we can always go to Jesus.

> *Can we find a friend so faithful,*
> *Who will all our sorrows share?*
> *Jesus knows our every weakness;*
> *Take it to the Lord in prayer.*

His hands are open and the only things he carries in them are scars.

Crazy Love

My niece, Jayme, was styling hair in her Sumner, Washington, salon when a woman came into the shop with a frightened look on her face. The elderly woman said she was picking some things up and was waiting in Tacoma for a ride when a guy she didn't know picked her up and was threatening her. He drove her to Sumner where she escaped from his car and into the salon. She apologized for any danger she might be bringing into the shop. Over and over she spoke her name to my niece while looking over her shoulder to the street where a car was parked at the curb, engine running. A man sat in the driver's seat.

She had a couple of bags filled with various memorabilia. She was a little disoriented, so Jayme asked her if it would be okay if she escorted her the block or so to the police station where she might feel safe. The woman allowed that would be a good idea. They stepped out of the shop and took a few steps in the direction of the police station and the woman, with purpose, would not look at the idling car on the curb with the man sitting behind the steering wheel. As they crossed the street, she asked my niece, "Has anything like this ever happened to you before?"

"No, it hasn't," Jayme said.

The woman said, "Me neither. And I am twice your age!" (My twenty-seven-year-old niece said she was more like three times her age.)

As they made their way step-by-step to the police station, the car that had been parked at the curb with the man in the driver's seat slowly followed them. The driver put the car in park, got out, and asked my niece where she was taking the woman. "To the police station," my niece replied. The man smiled and got back into his car. It was then that Jayme felt convinced this was a person familiar with the woman and breathed a sigh of relief. The main entrance to the police station was locked, so they went around to the side entrance. The woman saw the car again and slipped her arm into the crook of my niece's arm and said, "Don't look at him and pretend you know me." The man put the car in park and waited outside the police station. My niece remembered the content of the bags the woman carried. One had a photo album in it that was white and kind of glittery like a wedding album.

With the woman safe in the care of the police, Jayme walked back down to her shop and finished her day. When she got home her husband was asleep, but she woke him up with tears flowing down her face. She told him the story and asked between sobs, "When I'm crazy will you . . . will you take care of me?"

Groggily he said, "You're already crazy and I take care of you."

What a great question! When I'm crazy, will you take care of me? Sadly, that won't happen for some who read these words. That man in the car patiently waiting outside the salon in Sumner had made a promise and, for God's sake, he was going to keep it. That's old school, but that's good school.

Our souls can never reach full maturity with only the shallowness of "young love." There's something about old love that has gone through decades of battles, misunderstandings, heartaches and tragedies, and yet emerges as a mature love that is eternal. God's love. Somewhere right now God is thumbing through the photo album of your life, and mine. And though we may be confused for a moment, we are safe, secure, and deeply loved.

Even if for a moment we forget Him, he will never for a moment forget us.

Because we are . . . and forever will be . . . His bride.

God is Good

I was a member of a church a few years ago, and the person who did the welcome and announcements greeted everyone every Sunday morning with this statement, "God is good." Then he paused and waited for our response. "All the time," we said.

"And all the time," he said. "God is good," we all would conclude.

Do you know deep down, rock-solid, for dead sure, that the God you worship, the God you follow, the God you serve, is a good God? Theologians throughout the centuries have talked about the intrinsic goodness of God, which means in everyday language that all the good that God does in this world, and all the good He does in your life or in my life, flows out of this basic character and nature.

One day when Caleb was about six years old, he greeted me at the front door. He had a wry smile on his face and a twinkle in his eye that usually means mischief is not very far away. I looked at him and in a sweet and kind voice I said, "What do you want?" He asked, "Daddy, are you in a good mood?" I said, "I don't know . . . why?" He said, "Oh nothing. But will you tell me when you are in a good mood?" My son understood the limitations of his earthly father's goodness. He knew that he stood a better chance of receiving what he wanted if he caught me in a pleasant mood.

God, on the other hand, is intrinsically good. Catch him any hour of any day and rest assured you'll find Him good. It's His nature to be good. It's His approach to every day, every person, and every situation. Which is why in the creation account in the Book of Genesis, it should come as no surprise to any of us that God creates a good universe. He does a really good job. The skies, the seas, the plants, and the animals—all are good. And when he creates Adam and Eve, they're really, really good. Would anyone expect anything less from an intrinsically good God? You wouldn't expect a bad job from a good God.

Adam and Eve make some terrible choices. They rebel against God. Soon after, their children and grandchildren fall into evil of every sort: thievery, adultery, murder. So what does an intrinsically good God do when his good creation goes bad? He could walk away. He could wipe them out. On the contrary, our intrinsically good God puts a good plan together in order to stem the flow of violence and evil in the world.

> For God so loved the world that He gave His only begotten Son, that whoever believes in Him should not perish but have everlasting life. For God did not send His Son into the world to condemn the world, but that the world through Him might be saved.
> (*New King James Version,* John 3:16-17)

Nearly forty years ago Nette and I got married in Slidell, Louisiana. All of her family made the trip to the New Orleans area: Aunts, uncles, grandparents, and cousins. I was sitting in a living room chair one afternoon the week before the wedding reading and noticed Lynette's grandmother Maske, who was one of the most beautiful grandmothers I have ever seen, wiping down the counter in the kitchen. Grandma Maske had Alzheimer's. She never called my name, but she had the most wonderful smile that made her entire face disappear behind a flash of beautiful white teeth. She smiled, always. She was as sweet as powdered sugar.

Grandma Maske . . . I watched her mindlessly wipe down the counter in the kitchen, circles and circles in a familiar motion that she must have practiced for decades in her own Nebraska farmhouse where she lived most of her life. As I watched the lovely lady wipe down the counters, alone in the kitchen my heart broke for her. I ached to know her. I wanted to ask her questions about her granddaughter that I was about to marry. What was Nette like as a little girl?

Grandma Maske seemed so saintly. She seemed so peaceful. Was it just the effect of the disease? I felt a painful lump form in my throat as I watched her methodically move down the counter towards the window over the sink. Then as she got to the sink, she lifted her face and looked out the window—I imagine like she had done hundreds of times on the farm looking for her husband or watching the wind bend the wheat—and she began to sing only to herself and barely audible "God is so good. God is so good. He is so good to me..." Then she blinked, smiled and muttered something I couldn't make out. She took her gaze off the Nebraska fields of her memory and back to the counter top in Louisiana and restarted her circular motion to finish the job of cleaning a clean counter.

I was staggered by the implications. In that moment God told me that my life was going to be needlessly painful and full of disappointments if I didn't let go of bitterness and simply trust in the simple truth: God is good.

Oh, taste and see that the Lord is good!
(English Standard Version, Ps. 34:8*)*

I have.
And He is.

Pygmy God

I'm deeply convinced that the way we live is a consequence of the size of our God, and the problem that most of us have is that our God is too small. We are not convinced that we are absolutely safe in the hands of a fully competent, all knowing, ever present, utterly loving God who is so big.

Abraham had a big God. When He instructed Abraham to leave his homeland and move to an unknown country scripture says, "So Abram departed as the Lord had spoken to him" (*New King James Version,* Gen. 12:4). Moses had a big God. When he was caught between the devil and the Red Sea God said, "...Lift up your rod, and stretch out your hand over the sea and divide it. And the children of Israel shall go on dry ground..." (Ex. 14:16). David had a big God. When he was confronted by a giant named Goliath, he smiled, stooped and picked up five smooth stones saying, "the battle is the Lord's" (1 Sam. 17:47). Mary had a big God. When she was confronted with the prospect of birthing and raising the Son of God she conceded with the angel, "with God nothing will be impossible" (Luke 1:37-38). Saint Paul had a big God. He said from the damp prison in Rome, "I can do all things through Christ who strengthens me" (Philippians 4:13).

If I wake up in the morning and I go through the day with a shrunken God, there are consequences. I will live in a constant state of fear and anxiety because everything depends on me. My moves will be governed by whatever circumstances hit me that day. When I have a need, if I live with a shrunken God, I will find it unnatural to pray because I'm not really sure, to be honest, that God makes a difference and that prayer matters.

If you live with a shrunken God, one who does not offer divine, unconditional acceptance, you will pull your punches when you need to give somebody a strong word of confrontation or challenge. Then you become a slave to whatever other people think of you. If I face temptation to speak deceitful words to avoid trouble, I'll do it. Or if I can get credit for something at work that doesn't really belong to me, if I don't trust there's a God who sees in secret and then rewards one day, I'll do it.

When somebody gets mad at you or disapproves of you, you get all twisted up in knots. You won't have the security of knowing that if a giant God loves you, cares for you as your Father, then what difference does it make how people think you are doing?

When human beings shrink God, they offer prayer without faith, worship without awe, service without joy, and suffering without hope. The result is a life of stagnation and fear, a loss of vision, an inability to persevere and see it through. And it's against this backdrop that the writers of Scripture never tire of telling us, "You do not live with a little tribal God."

Whatever your need, God is bigger. Whatever your weakness, God is stronger.

> *Yours, O Lord, is the greatness,*
> *The power and the glory,*
> *The victory and the majesty;*
> *For all that is in heaven and in earth is Yours;*
> *Yours is the kingdom, O Lord,*
> *And You are exalted as head over all.*

(1 Chron. 29:11)

Rise Up

He went out and saw a tax collector named Levi, sitting at the tax office. And He said to him, "Follow Me." So he left all, rose up, and followed Him.

~ Luke 5:27-28

Simple call. Simple obedience. This meant Levi was apprenticing himself to Jesus. All of his decisions are filtered through the grid of the relationship with Jesus. Levi is now attached to Jesus.

Dietrich Bonhoeffer wrote in *The Cost of Discipleship*, "When we are called to follow Christ, we are summoned to an exclusive attachment to His person." Following Jesus means having an exclusive attachment to Him. That is the defining relationship for the Christian. Following Jesus is now the functioning control center of your entire life. Every other relationship is now transformed because of your relationship with Jesus.

When I married my wife, I made a decision to have an exclusive attachment to her and that attachment informed all future decisions. She influenced my career choices, how I spend our money, what I did for recreation, down to what I wear in public!

It works no less with Jesus. Notice Levi left his past behind. He thought about his vocation differently. He thought about relationships differently. Everything changed when he apprenticed with Jesus. Jesus refuses to be a fashionable accessory to a life in which you are still in charge. If you are a follower of Jesus, it means that you are not in charge of your life anymore. See, Jesus will be of supreme importance or he will be of no importance, but he will not be of some importance to you.

How is Jesus saying to you, "Follow Me"? I suggest we carve out some time with Him to let him shape our minds and souls. Further, I think it would be helpful to select a specific aspect of His teaching and press it into the depths of our hearts until it becomes an integral part of our lifestyle. That might be His teachings on conflict management found in Matthew 5 and 18. It might be his teaching on forgiveness found in Luke 7, or his teaching on worship found in John 4. How about giving found in Luke 19? Where in your life is Jesus saying, "Follow Me"?

The Jesus attachment means we go on mission with Jesus. Levi never got over his encounter with this Rabbi Jesus on that hot Palestinian day. He demonstrated it by throwing Jesus a party and introducing his friends to Jesus. We also know he went on to a best-selling writing career. His name was changed to Matthew and he wrote the first Gospel of the New Testament that bears his name. He was so moved by his attachment to Jesus he literally wrote the book on Jesus. He desperately wanted people to know that through a relationship with Jesus, they could be accepted and loved into the Kingdom of God. According to church tradition Levi/Matthew lived out his apprenticeship in such a way that it cost him his life. And when we "get grace" it will have the same effect on our lives. I should never "get over" the grace Jesus offers ragamuffin me. I wonder who in my world is sitting at a tax booth waiting to have an encounter with Jesus, and Jesus is just waiting for me to be his hand, eyes, and voice to tell them they are welcome in the Kingdom

Anne Lamott is an author and self-described hippy who lives in San Francisco. Her work can be profane, funny, and profound, often in the same sentence. Throughout her adult life she was addicted to drugs and alcohol. She made many mistakes in relationships and ended up raising a son without a father. To the great shock of all of her family and friends, she converted to Christianity. In her book *Traveling Mercies* she describes her encounter with grace and conversion to Christ: "I do not understand the mystery of grace only that it meets us where we are, but that it does not leave us where it found us." Jesus is ready to meet you where you are, but He will never be satisfied to leave you where He found you.

He comes to us as One unknown, without a name, as of old, by the lakeside, He came to those men who knew Him not. He speaks to us the same words: "Follow thou me!" and sets us to the tasks which He has to fulfill for our time. He commands. And to those who obey Him, whether they be wise or simple, He will reveal himself in the toils, the conflicts, the sufferings which they shall pass through in His fellowship, and, as an ineffable mystery, they shall learn in their own experience Who He is. (Albert Schweitzer, *The Quest of the Historical Jesus*)

What are you going to do when He calls?

Down Jericho Way

Sometimes there are medical reasons for the heaviness we carry in our hearts. Sadly, there are also dark days and heavy hearts that can't be treated by modern-day doctors. An ancient physician tells about a man who had many dark days in Jericho. Dr. Luke describes him as a tax collector and a bit undersized. Rumors were that Jesus was coming and the entire town turned out to see this miracle-working, Pharisee-defying rabbi.

Tax collectors in Jesus's day were government-sanctioned crooks, thugs in silk suits who arm-twisted merchants into handing over their hard-earned profits. Often, they falsified the tax bills and skimmed off the extra for themselves. Zacchaeus was such. He was "a chief tax collector," Luke says and adds the obvious: "and he was rich." Fine clothes lined his closets, ruby and emerald rings adorned his fingers. He was a prosperous businessman, and could buy anything his heart desired—anything, that is, but self-respect and the friendship of others.

Did he have sleepless nights? Did he ever wake up in the morning, see his wife sitting across the table from him and think, "She has no idea how sad I am on the inside"? In spite of his stoic demeanor, did the whispers of people passing in the market place sting and scar his heart? Then he heard Jesus was coming to town. Zacchaeus, perhaps, has heard how he befriended the lost and lonely, the outcast and castoffs. No matter that his externals were in place, Zacchaeus felt he didn't belong, felt like an outsider in his own home, among his own people. And so, he determines to see this Jesus.

As the procession passed by, Zacchaeus "sought to see who Jesus was, but could not because of the crowd, for he was of short stature" (*New King James Version,* Luke 19:3) This limitation never stopped him before from getting what he wanted, and it's not going to stop him this time either. He climbed a tree to get a better view. Think of this little rich man in his fine clothes shinnying up a tree to see Jesus. That must have been quite a sight. Jesus looked up through the leaves and called him by name and invited himself over for dinner. Shocking. Scandalous even. Polite rabbinical company did not associate with common riff raff.

The way Luke tells the story it was as if Jesus went to Jericho looking specifically for Zacchaeus. Jesus says, "I must stay at your house." In other words, Jesus was saying, "You are why I have come to this town, Zacchaeus. I didn't come for recreation. I didn't come to further my career. I came for you." To us it looks like Zacchaeus might be an interruption to the busy ministry of the Son of God. But Jesus lived life by a different rhythm. People were never interruptions to him. I love what Henri Nouwen wrote in *Reaching Out*:

> While visiting the University of Notre Dame, where I had been a teacher for a few years, I met an older experienced professor who had spent most of his life there. And while we strolled over the beautiful campus, he said with a certain melancholy in his voice, "You know...my whole life I had been complaining that my work was constantly interrupted, until I discovered that my interruptions were my work.

Zacchaeus was the work of Christ. And so are you.

What chases away a joyless day? What is the cure for a sullied and sorrowful heart bent only on serving self? Zacchaeus knew he was the object of affection of the Son of God. He was no interruption. The text says, "So (Zacchaeus) made haste and came down, and received Him joyfully" (Luke 19:6).

Jesus equals joy. This amazing revelation occurs when Jesus is received with joy. You begin to want to clean up your messes. You begin to consider making relational reparations. Zacchaeus stood and said, "Look, Lord, I give half of my goods to the poor; and if I have taken anything from anyone by false accusation, I restore fourfold" (Luke 19:8). From a heart full of joy, Zacchaeus made amends to those whom he had wronged. The people of Jericho could never have imagined this traitor would turn into such a generous soul. In his book *Intimate Moments with the Savior*, Ken Gire describes the amazing transformation of this man whose life, once stunted by greed, now flowed with generosity:

> From behind the barriers he has erected around his heart, a flood of repentant feelings bursts forth. Feelings that had been dammed up for years. Zacchaeus goes out on still another limb. What took a lifetime to accumulate, one sentence of devotion liquidates. And not by a token ten percent. Half to the poor. Fourfold to the defrauded.

On a recent run I felt a clear conviction that I owed two men some money. One man I had not seen for thirty-five years and was unaware he felt I owed him anything. The second one is a man I knew five years ago. We were business associates and the relationship ended with acrimony, both feeling wronged by the other. He called me the other day and asked if he could pick up a couple of old backpacks I had stored for him. I had given them away to Goodwill years ago. He was hurt by that, said I had no right to give away what was not mine in the first place. He's right, of course.

On my run I thought of these two men. Like an old west sawbones probing for a bullet and finally tapping something hard and unforgiving with his wand, the Holy Spirit said to me, "You will never balance the books in these relationships. But you can position yourself to clean up your conscience by making restitution, and when you do, you will remove the foreign object the evil one is using to bring an infection to your soul."

So, I bought a couple of money orders this week, stuck each into an envelope, and sent them down to Jericho.

Up There

"Listen to your life. See it for the fathomless mystery it is. In the boredom and pain of it, no less than in the excitement and gladness: touch, taste, smell your way to the holy and hidden heart of it, because in the last analysis all moments are key moments, and life itself is grace."

~ Frederick Buechner, Now and Then: A Memoir of Vocation

In December of 1980 or so, I wrote my father a note asking him about going into the ministry. I had sensed a "call" to preach at nine years old, but had found a lot of satisfaction and success as a young man working in the construction field and was confused about my vocation. I have kept his scrawl, on a worn and faded piece of paper, these many years. I share it now because my son is asking some of the same questions; maybe others are as well.

> Your call to preach cannot be based on whether or not you are happy working the job you currently have. God made all of us to be happy when we are productive. And you haven't been productive in a long while. Jesus is telling you that real joy comes when we have "entered into the joy of the Lord" which is being productive like God is productive. (cf. Matthew 25:14-31)
>
> A sense of fulfillment will come to you when you are productive. For God made us to cooperate with Him in stewarding this good earth. Your call to preach God's Word must come from God, not a feeling of satisfaction from within. It is a call to give up one's normal pursuits of life and make the wellbeing of the

Church of Jesus Christ your vocation.

God may want you to be a bi-vocational pastor or a lay leader in the Church, but the call comes from God not through reason or any sense of fulfillment in your current job. It is a call to build His Church.

Have a Merry Christmas,

Dad

Lynette and I were visiting the Plymouth Plantation in Massachusetts a few years ago and I had an interesting encounter with one of the actors participating in the interpretive museum. He was in one of the replica thatched-roofed huts and as we passed by, we could hear him reading scripture. Nette and I walked into "his" house and listened to him read from the book of Ecclesiastes. After a few minutes I asked him a question or two like what was the weather like and how was the voyage over on the Mayflower. The actor, speaking in a brogue accent, stayed in character the entire conversation. He portrayed one of the actual pilgrims that made the arduous trip. Curious as to what "Isaac's" trade in the New World was, I asked, "Isaac, what is your profession?"

With the 1611 version of the King James Bible open on his lap, he looked at me with incredulity and said, "Why I am a Christian, sir!" I smiled at the profundity of this actor and asked a second time what his trade was. He said that he was a tailor.

Calling and profession can be confusing. I know this: the Kingdom of God on this earth is the most important mission I can be a part of. I have been called to leave my "normal pursuit" of the world and dedicate myself professionally to preach and teach the Word of God. However, we all have a higher calling than that. All who are born from above have been beseeched to walk worthy of the calling to which we were called. We have all been called to be foot soldiers in the advancement of the kingdom of heaven. So, whether you work as a teacher, an engineer, a bricklayer, or a preacher, we are all called to be Kingdom-bringers to this sorry, dark world.

A job is an avocation and exists only to provide a means to

advance the vocation. And that calling, my friends, is to bring "up there down here."

That is my profession and it is yours as well.

Ten Thousand Charms

*On the third day there was a wedding in Cana of Galilee, and
the mother of Jesus was there. Now both Jesus and His
disciples were invited to the wedding. And when they ran out
of wine, the mother of Jesus said to Him, "They have no
wine." Jesus said to her, "Woman, what does your concern
have to do with Me? My hour has not yet come."*

~ John 2:1-4

Most thirty-something singles who attend a wedding at some
point imagine their wedding day. Is this happening for Jesus as
He watches the wedding feast at Cana of Galilee? He sees the
joy, His eyes dance and He laughs with everyone else. He hears
the music and He claps and sways to the strum of the
instruments, and perhaps He grabs His mother's hand and takes
her on a twirl around the dance floor. Maybe He's a little out of
breath from the dance; His face is flushed from the wine and as
He makes His way back to His seat says to himself, "I will have
a wedding one day. It won't be with a girl. It will be with a
people."

Then in an instant the bright joy is chased away by the dark
knowledge of what will have to happen to make that wedding
possible. Every time John uses the word "hour" in his Gospel,
he is referring to the crucifixion of Jesus. So, while everyone at
this gathering is celebrating a wedding, Jesus knows in order
for Him to go to His own wedding, He has to pass through a
funeral. That was what was on His mind.

As He puts the golden chalice to His lips to sip the new wine,
a single drop falls onto the white linen table covering and the
crimson spot begins to spread as the cloth absorbs the wine. He
knows that one day his blood must be spilled. The sweetness of

the joy of new-wine moment is traded for a sharp tang of the coming wine-soaked sponge on a hyssop branch.

He is very aware that there is a barrier between the Lover and the beloved. And He thinks, "If I am going to raise the cup of festive joy at my wedding feast, I am going to have to drink the cup of the Divine wrath of God. I have to go through that 'hour.' I will have to provide the wine, if I am ever going to have this spousal love with my Bride—my people. I have to pass through a funeral and the wine, my blood, must be spilled.

"I will strip naked for my beloved—on the cross.

I will offer my heart up to the point of breaking—on the cross.

I will be hacked to pieces so that my beloved will be restored—on the cross.

I will become ugly so that my beloved may become radiantly beautiful—on the cross."

When I see the extent and depth of love that occurred on the cross for me a promiscuous lover, it changes me; it makes me want to please my heavenly Lover. "For He made Him who knew no sin to be sin for us, that we might become the righteousness of God in Him" (*New King James Version,* 2 Cor. 5:21).

It doesn't really matter what a girl looks like in street clothes. In a wedding dress she is radiant; she is beautiful. You and I are not much to look at from an eternal perspective. In fact, I am not sure we could even say we are plain. From a holiness perspective, we are rather hideous, but we have a Groom who went to a funeral, and passed through that dark veil of death to welcome us into the bridal chamber today.

In His nail-scarred hands He holds the unspoiled linen of His righteousness ready to wrap around our sagging shoulders. He looks at us with the longing eyes of our heavenly Lover, and no matter what we look like in our street clothes we are beautiful to our Groom. So...

I will arise and go to Jesus,
He will embrace me in His arms;
In the arms of my dear Savior,
O there are ten thousand charms.

Saint Joe

This is a faithful saying and worthy of all acceptance, that Christ Jesus came into the world to save sinners, of whom I am chief.

~ 1 Timothy 1:15

Often people tell their pastor their dark secrets. I learned a long time ago to never say, "You've got to be kidding!" when someone reveals a deep dark sin. Can you imagine someone coming to the Apostle Paul and saying, "I get that God would love you, Paul. You are a church planter and Scripture writer; you are a good person, but I am not. God could never love someone like me, not after what I have done."

Paul could have said, "Are you kidding! Have you killed church people? Because I have...Jesus came into the world to save sinners, of whom I am chief." Paul is saying, "God is in the business of saving people who are a hot mess—and I am at the front of that line. So, if you are a mess-of-a-person, like me—then you are Jesus's kind of person." But, you say, Paul was a Pharisee and a good guy. Really?

What has helped me a great deal has been to take a long hard look at my sinful life in the mirror of God's word and let it drive me to the brink of despair. Then in that darkness, tune my ears to the whisper from the gentle Savior and hear him say, "Your sins are forgiven. Go in peace." It is amazing when I see the national-debt-size of forgiveness I have received; it makes me want to be a forgiver as well. When I am astonished at how much I have been forgiven, I desperately want to pay it forward to the hard-to-love people in my life.

I took a writing course a few years ago down in the Wallingford area of Seattle, WA. The first night we were there the instructor served us refreshments as we got to know one another—a meal of sorts. He was at the head of the oblong table and I was at the foot. There were probably fifteen people in the class.

He asked us to go around the table and tell our name, where we live, what we do for a living and what we want to write about. There was a computer programmer who wanted to write about espionage. There was a scientist who wanted to write a non-fiction book on the environment, a real estate agent who wanted to write about food and wine. Sitting next to me was a lady who said she was an office manager in downtown Seattle and wanted to write about sex. The group broke out in a chorus of oohs and ahhs. Then she went into some detail about the kind of erotica she planned to write.

My turn. "My name is Joe Chambers from Mukilteo and I want to write about my experiences in the wilderness." I turned my head to the next person indicating I was finished and for us to move along in the round robin. The group almost in unison asked me what I did for a day job. "I'm a pastor." The place erupted in laughter.

The office manager lady apologized profusely and leaned over to me and said, "I really am sorry, Father. I am not much of religious person. Please forgive my crassness."

Want to know what I said? "Well, my child, I'm not a very religious person either and neither is my church or Jesus. In fact our motto is: 'No perfect people allowed.'"

She said, "I think I could go to a church like that."

When Johnny Cash died a few years ago, director Tony Kaye got a bunch of celebrity singer-song writers and actors to lip-sync a Johnny Cash song called "God's Going to Cut You Down." It is in an edgy, grainy, black and white style. You see people like Sheryl Crow, Johnny Depp, Keith Richards, Kris Kristofferson, Chris Rock, and Denis Hopper lip sync along with the foot stomp and gravelly voice of Johnny. Right in the middle the video, Bono, of U2, stands up with a paint brush and scrawls as graffiti on a wall the words "Sinners Make the Best

Saints."

May the love of Jesus disturb, transform, and re-shape you—even you who are a mess—because in Jesus's eye, sinners make the best saints.

Stop, Look and Listen

Mary...sat at Jesus' feet and heard His word. But Martha was distracted with much serving... And Jesus answered and said to her, "Martha, Martha, you are worried and troubled about many things. But one thing is needed, and Mary has chosen that good part."

~ Luke 10:39-42

Mary serves as an example for all of us that to be Jesus' disciple means we slow down and live in deep friendship with God. The phrase "that good part" is a food term. It means the best part of the meal. The prime cut of meat. Martha was so distracted by her overcooked potatoes that she missed the meal of a lifetime—the good part of human existence is sitting in her living room sharing the Bread of Life.

Mary found soul satisfying sustenance at the feet of Jesus. How can I find that one thing needed? How can we learn what Mary learned? I think one way is by deliberately slowing down and placing ourselves in a position where we have to wait. Here are a few suggestions for slowing down:

For one month, drive in the slow lane.

Declare a fast from honking.

Twice a week cook a complete meal with fresh ingredients from scratch and without using the microwave.

For the next month, when you're at the grocery store, look for the longest checkout line. Get in it. Let one person go ahead of you.

Go through one day without wearing a watch.

You get the idea. Find ways to deliberately choose waiting,

107

ways that make hurry impossible. Don't worry that if you don't rush, you aren't being very productive. Researchers have found that there is no correlation between multi-tasking, Type-A behavior and productivity.

Another thing we could do is to practice sacred reading. We have more access to the teachings of Jesus in our generation than any in history and yet, survey after survey indicates that we are the most biblically illiterate. When I was growing up the number of versions of the Bible was roughly equal to the number of TV channels available. We had the King James Version and we had the Red Letter Version of the King James Version. Today we have versions too numerous to count. You can read it on your phone, tablet, iPad, listen to it, and even have it emailed to you every day. There is an app for it on your phone. And yet we don't feed on His Word. What if we learned to read it like it is a letter from a friend or a love letter?

I received an email from an author I admire who read my blog last week, and he said some very moving things about the story. I promise you, I have read and re-read and re-read that email many times. I am savoring it. What would happen if we did that with the book we say that we love? What if we read the Gospels, not for data, but read slowly and invited Jesus to be present during the reading. Slow down, chew your food, and assimilate the meat of the Word.

We could add listening prayer to sacred reading. Mary's posture is not rattling off her list of stuff she wants Jesus to do for her. She adores Jesus for who He is, not what He can do for her. When was the last time you sat down and didn't ask God for anything, but just enjoyed his presence? Becoming comfortable with silence is where depth of relationship occurs.

Mother Teresa walked in complete obscurity for decades before the world found out about her. Every day during those years of obscurity she prayed and communed before her Lord in silence. Then when she became famous, she continued her practice of silent adoration. She had a practice of giving away what she called her "Business Card." On the card were these words:

> The fruit of silence is prayer.
> The fruit of prayer is faith.
> The fruit of faith is love.
> The fruit of love is service.
> The fruit of service is peace.

She was interviewed one time and asked if she really prayed every day. She nodded that she did. The reporter followed up with the question, "What do you say to God?"

"Mostly I just listen."

The reporter grew cynical and wryly asked, "What does God say to you when you listen?"

She smiled and whispered, "He mostly listens, too."

The way out of the frenetic life is simple, but it is not easy. It takes willful intention. But when you fall in love, it isn't hard to adjust your behavior for your beloved. Build into your life practices that put you at His feet. While you are there, be still, listen, and know that He is God.

The Power of Our Obsessions

Thou shalt have no other gods before me.
Thou shalt not make unto thee any graven image.

~ Exodus 20:3-4

I tend to think that an idol is some sort of totem or carved image; however, an idol is anything elevated to such an extent that I get my significance or my security from it. It can be an evil thing like drugs, or a good thing such as family. God does not suffer competitive lovers lightly. Tim Keller reminds us that, "We are all governed by an overwhelming positive passion." I cannot replace an idol by turning away from it. I have to turn toward something.

In the book of Genesis, a young man named Jacob meets a young woman named Rachel and wants to marry her. He offers to work for Laban, her father, in order to win Rachel's hand. Laban loves this deal. *"So Jacob served seven years to get Rachel,* but they seemed like only a few day*s to him because of his love for her"* (Gen. 29:20, NIV). This is remarkable! Every single day for seven years Jacob doesn't just show up for work, he shows up with a song in his heart. Why did seven years seem like a few days to Jacob? He had an overwhelming positive passion.

Zacchaeus had an overwhelming passion for money. He was an Israelite who collected taxes for the occupying government of Rome. This treasonous behavior meant that he gave up reputation, community, friendship, honor, and integrity to get money. Then one day he met Jesus, and on that day, he said, "All right, I'm done with money. I'm going to pay back everybody I ever cheated four times what I cheated from them. Then half of everything I have, I'm going to give it to help the poor." What enabled him to be liberated from his idol of money? He found a new overwhelming, positive passion. His name was Jesus.

One of C.S. Lewis' friends, Dorothy Sayers, wrote mystery

110

novels. She was one of the first women to graduate from Oxford and is famous for the Lord Peter Wimsey stories. Peter was a detective and an investigator. Think Sherlock Holmes. They are wonderful to read and are dramatized on the BBC. One critic pointed out that if you read the Peter Wimsey stories closely, you can see that though he was successful at solving mysteries and crimes, he was lonely. He was a lonely bachelor. Halfway through the series of detective novels, a character is introduced named Harriet Vane. And guess what? She writes mystery novels and she was one of the first women to graduate from Oxford. Sound familiar? Dorothy Sayers had looked into her own creation and fallen in love with her hero. She saw how lonely he was, and so wrote herself into the story. She won his love; they got married. She saved him from his life of loneliness.

That is exactly what God did. He looked into the world He created and saw us flailing and floundering. He wrote Himself into the story as Jesus Christ who died on the cross to save us. When you grasp that, and let Him "win you over" and fall in love with Jesus, you will see your idol tarnish in the light of such love. You will cast it down and embrace Him. You must be willing to be "won over" and then, Jesus becomes your magnificent obsession.

Turn your eyes upon Jesus,
Look full in His wonderful face,
And the things of earth will grow strangely dim,
In the light of His glory and grace.

Love Finds a Way

When he was still a great way off, his father saw him and had compassion, and... said... "this my son was dead and is alive again; he was lost and is found."

~ Luke 15:20, 22, 24

We were camped at close to 10,000 feet in the mountains of Colorado near the Continental Divide in the fall of 1999. After a few days of hunting and not seeing many elk, my father and I needed to come out of the mountains Saturday evening to preach at our respective churches on Sunday morning. We left Jim, my best friend and associate pastor, in the mountains to continue his hunt. We would be back the next evening to continue our weeklong hunt in the mountains. All my life had been traveling to this moment. As a pastor, I had invested every ounce of my soul into being a preacher and a leader. It had become my reason for existing. I was good at both. Virtually everything could be taken from me, but I could always preach. I could lose my family, and yet I could still preach. I could lose my health, but I could still preach. I could lose my voice, but I could still preach, or write.

In Littleton on that Saturday evening, my world imploded. My infidelity had been discovered while I was in the mountains. The consequences were all waiting for me when I got home. An "intervention" had been arranged and was awkwardly handled. My wife took our three boys and moved in with her mother and father. I was left alone in our house. I resigned my position as pastor via an email to my staff, deacons and elders, and began to spiral down in darkness. The only thing I knew to do was to go back to the mountains. I have always been more at home in the mountains than anywhere. So I carried more provisions to my camp, packed up my tent and gear, and moved higher up into the mountains further away from where any man might go in the deep alpine snow. I had my gun and could kill what I needed to live; I had planned to stay for weeks up there.

Somewhere around day two or so I began to panic. My only means of making a living lost, how would I take care of my family? The currency of a pastor is his integrity and mine had been spent in prodigal sinning. Having placed all my intellectual and soul capital in what I performed for my identity, I was spiritually and relationally bankrupt. I lost hope and found despair. During this darkness I considered having a hunting accident and ending my life. Life insurance would take care of my boys and wife for years to come. Depressed, scared, angry, hurt, and alone, shame slammed me into the ground like an avalanche, crushing the life out of me. I could see no future. This way out would be quick and painless.

Painless … less pain … that is what I needed. Even in the immediate aftermath of my public humiliation, I thought about how I could ease my own pain. As I fell deeper and deeper into that hole of self-pity, my only thoughts were of myself, not my wife, my three young sons, or several hundred people who called me pastor. Personal pain-management was on my mind.

Thinking of my wife and sons and the joy that comes from being loved, I took the 7mm shells and threw them out into the three-foot-deep snow covering the ground in the dark timber at 10,000 feet. The next morning, I filled a light pack and climbed a 12,000-foot ridge to check messages on my cell phone. There were about ten, not all civil. There was a worried, plaintive one from my wife begging me to call her. Several were from angry people. However, there was one message from my father that changed everything.

As I listened to his message, I could hear the wind blowing in the receiver of his cell phone; he was breathing hard. His message said, "Son, I know that if you don't want to be found, I will never find you. But I just wanted you to know that I am up here, walking these ridges looking for you. I love you, son."

Above tree line, I sat down beside a cairn, a pile of stones, and wept. My tears froze to my cheeks and sent a chill down to my bones. I trekked down the mountain, packed up camp, and walked to the trailhead. Driving away, I saw my father arriving in his truck. Through my unzipped jeep window I asked what he was doing. He had come up every day—looking for me. I told him I was going home to see if I still had a wife. He asked if I wanted him to go with me to meet her, and I allowed that I did. He followed me two hours to Littleton.

That was over two decades, countless counseling sessions, and rivers of tears ago. Still, the bride of my youth is with me. We now enjoy the fruit of repentance, recovery, and forgiveness. In December of 2012, we celebrated thirty-one years of marriage.

Where did my wife learn to ache for me and beckon me to come home? Where did my sons learn to hope in the father hiding in the mountains? It was love; a love birthed in eternity, proven on an old rugged cross, and spoken through a scratchy cellphone. In the *Les Miserables* finale lyrics there is a stanza that says:

> *Take my hand*
> *And lead me to salvation*
> *Take my love*
> *For love is everlasting*
> *And remember*
> *The truth that once was spoken:*
> *To love another person is to see the face of God.*

Once you've felt that love in the depth of your soul, there is no place to go but home.

Part Four:

Notes from Suffering

The wound is the place where the Light enters you.

~ Rumi

Out of suffering have emerged the strongest souls;

the most massive characters are seared with scars.

~ Kahlil Gibran

If you don't forgive sins, what are you going to do with them?

~ Jesus

Pray Your Tears

About ten years ago I got a phone call that no one ever wants to get. My wife called me to tell me that my nephew and youngest son Caleb's best friend, Josh Bixler, had put a hand gun to his head and pulled the trigger at the age of fourteen.

I remember standing up and pushing my face into the corner of the room and screaming out to God. If someone had heard my guttural scream, they would have been certain that I had lost my faith. I had held this boy in my arms and dedicated him on Mother's Day. I had gone to his t-ball games. I had bought him Christmas presents. I had taken him backpacking several times with Caleb.

That evening, when we had to tell Caleb about the death of Josh, was one of the worst moments of my life. My wife and two oldest sons and daughter-in-law stood in our living room in a circle, held hands and prayed while fifteen-year-old Caleb was up in his room playing video games. I remember saying, "In five minutes Caleb will hear news that will send shockwaves into his soul for the rest of his life. He's upstairs as a child. After we tell him about Josh, he will go back up those same stairs—not a child."

The family asked me to eulogize Josh. I remember flying to Denver and feeling as if I were flying into a war zone. As I drove to Josh's house, dismembered memories lay like body parts at every street corner along the way.

I wrote as well as I could the eulogy that I wanted to share at the church in front of about 900 people, many of whom were students at Columbine High School. Yes, that Columbine High

School that had suffered so much horror seven years earlier.

What struck me was that while Josh's parents wanted to celebrate his life (and rightfully so), the music was a little too upbeat and cherry. The mood was a little too festive. People were clapping and smiling. The happier everyone got, the madder I became. My wife, as she does more than I would care to admit, reached over and patted me on my knee and said, "Easy does it, big guy. Easy does it."

The pastor called on me to come to the podium and share my eulogy. And the first thing I said was,

> This is not right. We, none of us, should be here. You students should be playing soccer or studying for tests. You teachers should be grading papers. Caleb should be watching a Star Wars movie with Josh. His parents should be at work. I should be at home writing a sermon. This is not what God wanted any of us to be doing today...

Well, that sucked the life out of the room.

We live in a culture that is clueless about how to grieve and cry out to God. We live in a celebratory culture that wants everything to be rainbows, daisies, and puppy breath.

Author Tara Owens put it wisely when she said,

> Our inability to feel and articulate the deep sorrow of our life causes us to only experience truncated joy. There is an equilibrium between the depth of sorrow experienced and expressed and the abiding joy that God wants us to know in our lives.

We have lost our ability to cry out to God because we refuse to allow ourselves to feel deeply our hurt, doubts, pain and suffering. In short, we have lost the skill of lamenting.

It might surprise you that prayers of lament show up quite a bit in the Bible. And these are anything but pious, proper, or polite.

For example, in Psalms 13:1 we read: "How long, O Lord?

118

Will You forget me forever?

How long will You hide Your face from me" (*New King James Version*). Or we read in Psalms 44:23, "Awake! Why do You sleep, O Lord? Arise! Do not cast us off forever." Or in Psalms 39:13 the writer wants God to go away... "Remove Your gaze from me, that I may regain strength, Before I go away and am no more."

The question that a thinking person might ask is simply this, "What are these prayers doing in the Bible? And how do you and I make sense of them?" I think that these dark prayers of lament, that turn up more frequently than we might expect in this old prayer book, illumine for us a profound paradox about Christian praying. Praying your doubts, your tears, your anger, and your desperation is not a sign of a LACK of faith; it is an ACT of faith. Christian prayer takes seriously that life for all of us, sooner or later, can be hazardous to our health.

These words give us a vocabulary to yell for help to the living God when we are in the middle of our own troubles, vulnerabilities, anger, and confusion. The psalms of lament give us words to speak to God smack in the middle of our messy lives.

Why does an infant cry? It cries when it is hungry or when it has soiled itself. Those cries can be loud and incessant. The cries in the middle of the night are for help with some kind of discomfort. It is altogether appropriate for that infant to cry out under those conditions. What we learn from the ancient prayer book is that when we have "soiled" our lives and are sitting in our own filth, we can cry out to the living God and know that he hears us and will come to us. The fact that these laments are recorded in the book that we love, tells us that it is altogether appropriate for us to cry out under all conditions.

What does this mean for us practically? We can give God our tears.

In the Russian novel, *Brothers Karamazov*, there are a number of scenes in which Ivan, one of the brothers, shakes his fists at the heavens. Ivan is deeply troubled by the suffering of the world and, in particularly, of children. He protests over and over again: if there is a God, how could there be such horrific suffering in the world? If you read the novel it is telling that Dostoevsky, who is a Christian, offers no rhetorical answer to any of Ivan's questions. The counterpoint in the story is supplied by various characters' examples of love and faithfulness amid suffering.

I mention this because in the tapestry of Holy Scripture, the very same thing happens. Like it or not, the Bible offers to us less than we want on the one hand, but more than we could ask for on the other, in response to all of our protests and questions over life's hardships and the world's horrors. As products of the age of enlightenment we are prone to want answers. We want explanations. We are looking for cause and effect. So, when there is evil, horror, and suffering that defies our ability to understand, and we start looking to God for answers, we want him to give us solutions and explanations that make sense to us.

But when you turn to the Bible you don't find explanations as to why there is so much suffering in the world. What the Bible does is tell us a story. A long epic story about what God has done to rescue us; to rescue the cosmos. He does it by entering into it and coming near to us to taste our suffering and our hardship.

The scriptures don't settle for what God could say; they narrate for us what God does.

He does not snap his divine fingers and make it all go away; He dares to come near us in our plight. Jesus willingly gives himself to be "eaten up" in our suffering and death. The world's deep suffering closes in on Jesus; so that God can rescue us from the inside; from all of the dark and the wrong that swallows us up. In that way, we can be sure that, though it feels like our feet often slip in life and that we are in up to our necks, we are never in up to our necks—alone.

When your throat is dry from crying out to the heavens, and your eyes are swollen from weeping and looking around for where God might be hiding—here's where to look…

The Cross.

When you wonder to yourself, "Where is God in my heartache?" Lift up your head and look at the cross. The cross of Jesus is where the God of the universe has stepped in to the world, tasted the horror of suffering, dealt with the injustice of unpunished wrongs, and promised that He will bring us through it all.

There was an Andre Crouch song that was popular when I was a kid that said:

> *I've been to lots of places,*
> *I've seen a lot of faces,*
> *there's been times I felt so all alone.*
> *But in my lonely hours,*
> *yes, those precious lonely hours,*
> *Jesus lets me know that I was His own!*
> *Through it all,*
> *through it all,*
> *I've learned to trust in Jesus,*
> *I've learned to trust in God*

When we cry out to God in lament, God does not respond with quick fixes and pat answers. He responds by giving us Himself.

Bitter Him Than Me

What we relinquish to God, He accepts and changes.

Bitterness is hard to destroy. God's Spirit must be given the freedom to act, and He can't act in you without your permission. Paul wrote, "Let all bitterness ... be put away from you" (*New King James Version,* Eph. 4:31). That's hard. But God gives us the power to do it. If God is sovereign (and He is), if He loves you (and He does), and if you have done everything you can (and sometimes you have), then don't do anything more. Simply be still.

Jesus' final shout on the cross was, "It is finished!" That was a shout of relief and joy. Among other things, He was saying, "I have faced and experienced all that the Father has given, and praise the Father, it is over." You see, when you are hanging on a cross you can hardly do anything except hang on the cross. The nails won't let you get off, and the pain won't let you cover it with clichés. Crosses, though excruciatingly painful, provide some of the greatest joy in this world once they are accepted and experienced.

Several years ago I went through some of the most trying days of my life. My dad and I were in a deep relational conflict. I was driving to meet him for a week of bow hunting in the mountains of Colorado to try to talk him out of it. It was late at night and on the way to the camp, I got lost on an old logging road and was running low on gas. I began to think about how I could get some white gas out of my camping stove before I ran out when I down shifted and snapped the stick shifter off inside the console. I couldn't believe it. I was so furious that I ripped the console off the floorboard and found that I could still shift the one-inch nub. Feeling anxiety rising in my soul, I resumed my journey to the camp.

I was almost there and traveling entirely too fast for the rugged terrain, when I hit a rock in the road. That jarred the jeep so hard it bent the rim on my right front tire and knocked my battery out of its place over onto the alternator where the fins acted as a skill saw and cut a gash into the side of the battery. Battery acid sprayed everywhere, creating steam as it hit the hot engine block. But I was there.

We decided to be in the woods before sunrise the next morning; however, in my hurry to leave Denver I hadn't taken time to buy a hunting license. I had planned to go down to Meeker the next day to buy a bow hunting license, but it was opening day and I decided to go with my dad on the first hunt of the season and then go to town in the afternoon. The odds of me killing an animal were negligible and the possibility of being caught without a license this far back in the woods was very low. We set out about 4:00 in the morning. We didn't see any deer all morning and around mid-morning decided to go back to camp for breakfast.

As we topped a little hill there was a green game warden truck parked at a gate. When we got close, he asked to see our hunting licenses. Of course my dad got his out and I froze. I didn't have one. The game warden checked my arrows for blood and hair and was going to write a ticket for hunting big game without a license, which carries a $750 fine and no hunting for years in Colorado. I was embarrassed and ashamed. Eventually he reduced the ticket to hunting small game without a license, a much less severe penalty.

Back at the hunting camp over breakfast, my father and I tried to reconcile our differences. We were not successful. I was frustrated, angered, and disappointed. I could feel bitter bile rising in my soul. It was a dark time.

As I was leaving the camp and coming down the mountain, I turned a corner and hit an oncoming Nissan Pathfinder head-on. No one was hurt, but I couldn't drive my jeep. The entire front end was caved in. I had to walk about a mile back up to the hunting camp. I was embarrassed to ask for a ride down to a payphone to call for a tow truck and the Colorado State Highway Patrol. The officer cited me with a traffic violation and gave me a ride into Meeker.

It was a Saturday evening and I was scheduled to preach the next morning, so I needed someone to make the three-hour drive to come get me. I called for my ride and went to a café to get a bite to eat, drink coffee, and study my sermon notes for the next morning. Breathing deeply, I asked God's forgiveness for breaking the law—thought about the events of the last few days, the trauma, the disobedience—my dad's and mine—my poor jeep. Finally, I muttered, "Jesus! I just hand it all over to you. This is beyond me." And then I started laughing. If you had been there you would have thought that I had finally and completely lost my mind. I laughed until tears rolled down my cheeks. It wasn't bitter laughter, nor was it the laughter of cynicism. It was a free and freeing laughter. What else could I do? When I finished laughing, I noticed a difference. My situation was still as bad as it had been before. Nothing had changed…except me.

Satan hated my laughter. His plans were thwarted by it. He wanted to make me bitter. But because the laughter reflected my acceptance of suffering, he was the bitter one.

Bitter him than me!

From the Mouth of a Fool

When words are many, transgression is not lacking,
but the prudent are restrained in speech.

~ Proverbs 10:19

Look back on your years as far back as you can. What were the most breathtaking, exhilarating, emotion-producing 300 seconds you ever experienced?

I think I could make a good case that if you'd been able to talk about it at the time, the most exciting five minutes of your life would be the very first five. After nine months of darkness and isolation, you discover there's a whole world out there full of colors and tastes and sounds and sensations and other people. You discover you've entered into a realm beyond your wildest imaginings.

I think if you could have talked you would have said something like, "Mom, Dad, I had no idea! I actually had some reservations about leaving the womb. But now I see that this is a much better arrangement. I wouldn't have missed this for anything." It's very possible that the most exciting five minutes of your life were the first five minutes after you were born. It's all just been downhill ever since those five minutes.

But I believe that's nothing compared to what's to come. I think the most amazing five minutes you will ever experience will be the first five minutes after you die.

For centuries, the brightest minds that have ever lived have devoted whole lifetimes to try to penetrate what lies beyond that veil. They've tried to learn, "What is it that lies on the other side of death?" And five minutes after, you will know.

Those five minutes will happen for every one of us. Think about the sights that you're going to see, the sounds that you will hear, the experience that you will have in your first five minutes of eternity.

One of the most attractive things about those next "first five minutes" will be that I don't have to regret words that I have spoken. Rude words I've spoken to my wife. Careless words I have spoken to my sons. Unkind words I have said about friends. And out-and-out hateful words I have uttered about President Trump.

How often do you say something now and then you wish so much you could take it back?

Recently I shared a meal with a friend. We caught up on our respective summer activities. Then I asked him how he was doing. And he began to share with me about a particular physical ailment that he was experiencing. He said, "Joe, I don't know how to pray about it. I don't want to lose my eyesight. I want to continue to work. It really has me…"

"I know what you mean about not knowing how to pray about something," I interrupted.

Then I told him a 5-minute story about me. When I was finished he said, "Well, anyway I'm trying figure out how to pray about it and how to be with the reality of my body failing me."

Our breakfast ended, but that conversation has haunted me. Why did I inject a Joe-story when that man was sharing his heart with me? I failed my friend. Instead of being present with him and entering into his story of confusion and uncertainty, I told him one of my experiences. I thought about it all the way to Denver on a date with my wife. I thought about it while watching the film "War for the Planet of the Apes." I thought about it on the drive back from Denver.

I wrote my friend a note asking him to forgive me for not paying attention to his heart by filling up the space between us with my own words. He said he forgave me.

Thank God.

Ever wish you could just go back to a conversation and hit the "delete" button? Imagine never having to feel that regret

126

again. The first five minutes in heaven there will be no gossip, no sarcasm, no manipulating. Your heart will be full of affection and courage. I'm telling you, it will be the greatest five minutes of your life. And then the next five minutes will be greater. Then the next five will be greater, and that will be eternity.

And one of the reasons it will be so wonderful is the promise from the last book of the Bible that describes the truth about the nature of a Christ-follower in heaven. *"In their mouth no lie was found; they are blameless"* (*New Revised Standard Version,* Revelation 14:5)

Thank God.

Speed Bumps

I sat down on a cold plastic chair in a narrow beige room. A thick barrier of Plexiglas spanned the table to the ceiling. Tender names of lovers and vulgar epithets were etched into it alongside one another without shame. Loud voices and the bang of heavy metallic doors echoed in this cramped space as I waited for my friend to step through the door on the other side of the plastic barrier. In the two minutes that passed before he arrived, I replayed the high points of our friendship. I remembered the grace with which he received my story of sinfulness. The image of working side by side in a little church on Saturday Work Days flashed through my mind. The deep belly-laughter we enjoyed while telling stories with our families caused me to smile once again. I remembered the Bible study he led, the prayers he prayed, and his acts of service for the community. All of these memories tumbled together in a swirl of kaleidoscopic colors and shapes.

The door opened and in walked my friend wearing a pink jumpsuit. His eyes fell when I smiled at him. The smile on his face was an ambivalence of joy at seeing me, and shame at the same time. He said, "I am sorry, Joe. I am sorry you had to see me here in this place." Tears filled his eyes. "But," he continued, "I am glad you came to see me." I don't remember what I said, something about how cute he looked in pink. We tried to laugh. But laughter only covered our tears. Sadness and joy filled that confined space and became the sacrament of community. We handled those tender elements with great care. I prayed for him and promised to return the next week and every week until he was released. I kept that promise. Each week it got easier to talk with him about his life in prison and the complications of what put him there.

He told me that he remembered God speaking to him through

one of my sermons. He said, "Joe, do you remember when you preached about Samson? You talked about how he broke each vow one-by-one on his way to ruin. Each vow was like a speed bump God put into his life to cause him to slow down and consider what he was doing, but each time he approached a speed bump he just gunned the engine. Eventually he lost everything and ended up in prison chains. I heard you say all of that while I was careening out of control and thought *that won't happen to me. I'm a good driver.* Now, here I am in jail wearing a pink jumpsuit. I should have slowed down."

I heard a quote this week that said, "People want you to fix in a counseling session what they've rejected in a sermon." I wonder what I've heard in a sermon recently and chosen to reject. Maybe I didn't like the preacher. Maybe I didn't like the topic. Or maybe, I just decided I would enjoy the sin a little longer. I've done that.

Here's what I know: Sin will take you places you never dreamed you would go. It took Abraham to a lie about his wife. It took Moses to the desert. It took Samson to blindness. It took King David to Bathsheba. It took Peter to a warming fire. It took the prodigal to a pigpen. It took my friend to jail. Where is my sin taking me?

Here is the good news: There is no lie that God won't forgive. There is no desert that God won't cause to bloom. There is no infidel's bed that God won't purify. There is no fireside betrayal that God won't exchange for a breakfast fire of restoration. There is no pigsty that God won't redeem. There is no prison that God won't visit.

Just ask my friend in the pink jumpsuit.

There is therefore now no condemnation for those who are in Christ Jesus.

~ Romans 8:1

You Matter

Madalyn Murray O'Hair, the outspoken atheist who was instrumental in getting prayer removed from public schools, seemed, on the surface, to be tough as nails. Yet, recently her journal was uncovered and numerous times she had written, "Somebody, please love me."

People will do just about anything, in order to feel loved. Some people think, "If I succeed enough, people will love me," or "If I sleep with this person, he or she will love me," or "If I am pitiful enough, people will feel sorry for me and begin to love me." The problem is, none of these strategies work. Those who pursue love by means of success usually end up feeling used and unappreciated. The same can be said for those who try to trade sex for love. Those who use pity as a means of earning affection usually find that pity soon turns to contempt, and they end up feeling alone and abandoned.

I have discovered that most people who feel unloved have a distorted view of reality. They aren't really completely unloved; they just don't recognize the love that is in their lives. Their emotional pain blinds them to the fact that they have friends and family who love them very much. I want to say this to you. If you sometimes feel unloved, or if you really are in a position in life where there is no one at all who loves you, there is hope for you today.

Most of you have heard of Kurt Cobain. He was in the band Nirvana and he single-handedly started a new trend in the world of rock music; it was called "Grunge" music. He sold millions of albums, he had millions of fans, and the critics loved him. He had a beautiful wife and a daughter. Then, on April 5, 1994, he committed suicide. After it happened I saw an interview with a psychiatrist on CNN, and the question was asked, "How could a man who was loved by so many reach such a level of despair?" The psychiatrist said, "The adoring fans were a very small part of Kurt Cobain's life. His misery was caused by the fact that he felt estranged from the people that mattered most."

If you feel unloved, there is a hope I can offer you today. There is someone who loves you, and he matters very, very much. He has gone to amazing lengths to prove it.

God loves you.

You have heard that statement thousands of times throughout your life, maybe so many times that the statement has lost some of its impact. Some people think, "Yeah, God loves me. So what? He has to; He loves everybody." I want to make something clear. God loves you with all of His heart, and it's not because he got stuck with you. He doesn't love you just because you're part of the big mass of humanity. He loves you individually. He loves you as if you were the only one in the world to love. No matter what you have done, or no matter what your life has been like, God loves you. He wants to share His love with you. "The Lord did not set His love on you nor choose you because you were more in number than any other people, for you were the least of all peoples; but because the Lord loves you" (*New King James Version,* Deut. 7:7-8).

The Lord loves you.

Need proof? "Greater love hath no man than this, that a man lay down his life for his friends" (*King James Version,* John 15:13)

Look at the cross.

Beyond this, God cannot go.

The Beauty of Tears

And behold, a woman in the city who was a sinner, when she knew that Jesus sat at the table in the Pharisee's house, brought an alabaster flask of fragrant oil, and stood at His feet behind Him weeping; and she began to wash His feet with her tears, and wiped them with the hair of her head; and she kissed His feet and anointed them with the fragrant oil.

~ Luke 7:37-38

Why is the woman weeping? Our automatic assumption about tears is that something is hurting. Is that always true? I recently watched a video of a young mother singing a lullaby to her tiny baby and, while smiling, baby-tears streamed down the little chubby cheeks of that baby.

Many years ago, my wife and I were watching a television program that showcased young prodigies in various artistic disciplines. I believe I was reading a book while she watched. I heard a violin, a piano, and then I heard the voice of an angel. I looked up and saw a young Charlotte Church singing Andrew Lloyd Webber's "Pie Jesu."

Breathtaking. I glanced over at my wife; she was weeping. I had never seen her weep like that before. In a whisper, I asked if she was okay. "Beautiful, ," she mouthed to no one in particular. What is going on there?

I believe something in our soul aches for beauty. We were created with an insatiable desire for the indescribable. A paradox of painful beauty exists when we look at the darkness of our hearts and the grace that has washed it whiter than snow. There is the wonder of the Grace-giver who wraps us in the purity of that radical acceptance.

Let me tell you something from firsthand experience: Tears

132

often accompany repentance. Tears of grief fall for the pain we might have inflicted on loved ones from our selfish behavior. Those tears need to flow. We need to taste the salt of those tears on our tongue. Proof that repentance has done its deeper work of character change occurs when, after we turn away from our idols, selfish strategies and sin, another flow of tears comes—tears of joy. Psalms 30:5 says, "Weeping may endure for a night, but joy comes in the morning" (*New King James Version*).

There is a scene in the film *The Mission* that, to me personally, is one of the greatest moments in all of cinema. Robert DeNiro plays a slave trader in colonial Latin America. He had dedicated himself to capturing Indians and selling them as slaves. Jeremy Irons plays a Jesuit missionary who helped convert the Indians, and who defended them.

When DeNiro is thrown in prison for murder, Irons shows him mercy, and ransoms him to serve in the jungle mission. DeNiro insists on making the long journey to the mountain mission dragging his armor in a bundle behind him. He drags the weight of his sin and his filth to the top, where he meets the same people whose families he had pressed into slavery, now Christians. If they kill him, justice would be served.

As DeNiro is on his knees in the mud with the burden of his past tied to his back, the chief gives an order. Someone picks up a knife and runs to DeNiro and pulls his head upward with his face pointing to the very people he had hunted down like animals. The knife flashes and glints in the sunlight as the chief gives another order, and the knife cuts the rope to the burden on DeNiro's back. It tumbles over waterfall hundreds of feet, the same waterfall he had just climbed. He is confused. He looks into the faces of his former enemies for understanding. One by one, they begin to laugh, not the laughter of contempt, but the laughter of forgiveness and delight. Suddenly the face etched in pain and agony for all the guilt of his selfish life begins to melt away to first a smile, then a grin, and finally an open-mouth laugh of joy.

Never fear repentance; it is the pathway to change and joy. The great 19th century preacher Charles Spurgeon once said, "Blessed is the man who kisses the rod after having been smitten by it." God treasures the tears of repentance. They are His precious jewels. They cost so much: The price of our pain when we walked away from Eden. The pain of the cross when Jesus walked up a dusty road to a gnarled hill called Calvary and died to bring life, love, and beauty to a creation designed to pulse with beauty.

You number my wanderings; Put my tears into Your bottle.
~ Psalms 56:8

Father, Help Me!

Many years ago the phone rang and a familiar voice said, "Pastor, this is Dorothy. The doctors say Don won't make it through the night and he is asking for you." I told her I would be right there. I got dressed, put a ball cap on, brushed my teeth, and jumped in my jeep to head to St. Joseph's hospital in downtown Denver.

Don was a thin man when he was healthy; his respiratory illness had withered him still. He reminded me of the actor Hume Cronyn. He was a kindly and soft-spoken man. I never heard a cross word come out of his mouth. He and his wife were faithful, loving, and loyal members of the church. They were favorites. But after all the prayers and steroid treatments, Don's lungs were filling with fluid and growing weaker by the day, and then the hour, and now the minute.

As I drove downtown my mind raced for words of comfort, verses of scripture, lines from hymns, prayers I might offer. I asked God to give me words to help. I felt a need to be infused with wisdom beyond my years and answers beyond my education. Somewhere on Sixth Avenue, a thought entered my brain like a serpent. I don't know how it got in there. Maybe it had been there all along and just needed the warmth of this pastoral moment to stick its head out of its hole. But slowly and surely it slithered its way to the forefront of my mind and curled up there as if to give warmth—or maybe to take warmth in a reptilian way. *They didn't call anyone else, Joe. They only called you. He wants you to help him pass through to the other side. See, you are somebody.*

If you read that again, you can hear a hiss. I felt a swelling in my heart: Pride. I sat straighter in the seat. I hung my hand over the steering wheel and did my best to look cool and official in the darkness of that early morning drive to the hospital. No one was there to see the swelling of my chest or tilt of my head. It was just me, that hissing thought, and the presence of the Holy Spirit. How could I siphon off the energy from this tender moment and use it for ego-enhancement? I was disgusted with myself. At the parking lot and with every step to the glass doors and inside the elevator, I prayed that God would forgive my macabre and inflated sense of self-importance at the death of a saint and replace it with something to say or do that would help bring comfort.

My breath grew short and shallow and my mouth went dry as I entered the room. The hum of machines was muted and the smell of the hospital was stringent. I was filled with awe. My ego was hiding in its hole; after all, it is a coward in the presence of eternity, and death was ripping a portal into that eternal realm right there in the room with Don. Soon the Holy Spirit would scoop up this saint and take him home. This is no place for the trivial. I prayed the only words that came to me, "Father, help us." I couldn't remember any scripture, hymns, or poems. My head was an empty vault. That's all I had. I repeated it over and over. "Father, help us." I put my arm around Dorothy and held Don's hand until his chest quit rising and falling, and he died.

We stayed in the room as long as the medical staff would allow. Then they asked us to step outside. I held Dorothy while she wept in my arms in the harsh light of the hospital corridor. We walked to the little side room where various members of the family were waiting and weeping. I told her I would inform the prayer chain at church and we would begin the planning of meals. She nodded and thanked me for coming and went to each family member, one by one, and they hugged and wept. I watched from the hallway as an outsider now. It was okay. Don was in better hands and so was Dorothy.

Inside, my heart is a toxic cocktail of grace and ego. I am a needy pastor who needs to be needed and at the same time, a dispenser of the grace of the living God. For the life of me, I do not understand why God chooses to use such dirty vessels to dispense the elixir of heaven—but He does.

Rest in Hope

What do we call the kind of clock that's supposed to wake you up in the morning? An alarm clock! That's not a real optimistic name. It would be nice if we called it the opportunity clock or the resurrection clock, but we don't. The purpose of the buzz is to wake you up. Once you're awake, you turn it off.

I want to make an important distinction between two experiences—alarm vs. chronic anxiety. An alarm is a strong initial feeling of unpleasantness or concern designed to alert you that something's wrong and motivate you to take action. Imagine if a buzzer went off, you woke up, and never turned it off. You carried that buzzing sound with you all day. You go down for breakfast, it's still going on; you drive to work, you're not listening to the radio, the alarm is still going on. Moment by moment, hour by hour, all day long that sound does not stop.

There are people who live with chronic anxiety eating away at their heart and soul and it is more toxic by far than it would be to live with that annoying sound all day. I love what the Big Fisherman said "casting all your care upon Him, for He cares for you" (*New King James Version,* 1 Pet. 5:7)

Some well-meaning, but uninformed, soul says, "I thought that if you were a Christian, you didn't have any fear or burdens to cast on God! I thought we had no need to worry." When people have asked me if a Christian can suffer from emotional problems, I say, "Are you kidding? I'm close to a nervous breakdown myself!" When Christians are stuck with pins they bleed. Christians get cancer and die. Their kids do drugs. They go through divorce. Their businesses sometimes fail. Christians aren't exempt from anything, except hell.

A lady told me one time, "Joe, I could stand this if I knew it mattered to somebody—that anybody cared." The good news of the Gospel is that it does matter to God. Now, that doesn't mean it hurts less. That doesn't mean that you won't bleed, or get wounded, or get sick and die. You're exempt from nothing! But it does mean that every tear you shed matters to God and you can give it over to Him. No matter how bad it gets, we have a promise from God's Word that He will lift us up.

When I was about five years old, my family lived in Zephyr, Texas. Our house had a field out back that pastured two old, mean, gnarly rams. My brother, who was four or so, and I were forbidden to play in the field with the rams. My dad reminded us that they were mean and dangerous. He knew about these things, for my dad knew all things. He should have known it might not be a good idea to forbid young boys from exploring a dangerous field. It arouses something primordial in our DNA. We will defy all thoughts of safety and boldly go where no four- and five-year-old have gone before.

We had a blast exploring the creek that wound through the mesquite grove. We fought epic battles and defended our positions and won the day. When our last foe was vanquished, we made our way back to the fence that bordered our back yard. In that part of the field, there were two wood pallets set on edge to form a solid corner and a makeshift ladder over the fence. After my little brother had scaled the fence, it was my turn. My hand was on top of the wood when I heard snorting from behind. I wheeled about and saw I was face-to-face with the old, mean, gnarly rams. They were mad. They shook their heads and blew snot out of their noses. I started to cry; these were not pretend enemies, they were real. With his head lowered, the biggest one hit me full on in the stomach, slamming me against the wooden corner. I screamed as if this were a dragon blowing fire into my face. The ram backed up and charged again, slamming me a second time into the wood. What did my brother do? Did he try to come to my rescue? Did he try to fight off the demon sheep? Did he give me advice and counsel? Did he pray for me? Did he call out for help? No, I'll tell you what the little redheaded kid did; he screamed bloody murder like the four-year-old that he was.

I am smiling as I write this, now fifty years after the attack, but I will tell you I was scared out of my mind at the time. I had never been attacked by a demon sheep before and believed I was going to die. Suddenly, in the midst of that horror, as the ram was charging in for the kill, I felt a strong hand grab the back of my collar and pull me up with such force that the ram missed me and head-butted the wooden barrier instead. I saw blue sky as I rocketed upward and then felt two strong arms squeeze me tightly until the tears stopped. It was my father. 1 Peter 5:6 tells us "Humble yourselves, therefore, under God's mighty hand, that he will lift you up in due time" (*New International Version*).

Think about what really keeps you awake at night. Maybe it is a medical problem, perhaps it is your kids, or you wonder if you'll ever get married, your job, money, nobody loving you—it could be anything. The Father says to you, "Child, just be still. Toss those things over here and go to sleep. There's no use both of us staying up all night."

Pain as a Teacher

Nothing pierces the human heart like beauty and affliction.

~ Simone Weil

I consider myself a life-long learner. If there is one thing I do exceptionally well, it is that I gather information. Wild and random quotes float in my brain like dust motes on a beam of light splashing through a window. I know trivia that I, for the life of me, can't figure out why I know. For instance, I know that George C. Scott starred in a movie called *The Day of the Dolphin*. I have never seen the movie and don't know what it is about. I am not sure I have ever lost at the board game Trivial Pursuit. I have answers to questions no one is asking. The location of quotes in a book? I remember that it was in the third paragraph from the bottom on the right side of the book about a third of the way through the volume—chapter 5—and sure enough, the quote is right there. I worked for a pastor who would shout out from his office, "Where is that story about Jepthah and the strange sacrifice?" I would shout back, "Judges 11." He would say, "How do you know that?" I don't know. I remember my phone number from when I was a kid—2669—and that of my best friend, Tim—2389.

You might ask me a question and I won't know the answer, so don't think I am saying this because I am smart. I have never been accused of being smart. A smart aleck maybe. My wife says I have more worthless information in my head than anyone she knows. A friend told me one time, "Joe, you read so much to cover for the fact that you don't know anything." Exactly. My brother told me one time, "You only know what you read." Exactly.

Here is something that I know and didn't read in a book: Pain is the best and only way some people learn anything of deep soul-value. Abraham learned something about faith when God commanded him to sacrifice Isaac. Isaac learned something about trust on the three-day walk up to Moriah. Jacob learned about the transcendence of God at a river called Jabok, and he limped for the rest of his life because of it. David learned about forgiveness through the sin of adultery. John the Baptist learned about humility by being thrown into prison. Paul learned about the sufficiency of God's grace through a thorn in his flesh.

If it is true of those bright lights in the Christian firmament, it is certainly true for a dimwit like me. I learn best through the pain of my life. Don't get into a pasture of angry rams; they will charge a five-year-old boy. Don't dangle your leg in front of an open flame gas stove with flammable flannel pajamas; your leg will catch on fire. Don't swing out on a tailgate chain standing on the back bumper of a pickup going thirty-five miles an hour; the chain will break and you will go sprawling and spinning like a top on a dirt road. Don't date the school bully's girlfriend; he will come after you. Don't fail to show up for a court date, even if it is only a traffic violation; they will issue a bench warrant for your arrest. Don't go cross-country skiing wearing cotton socks; you will get frost-bite and lose the end of your toe. Don't cheat on a test; you will get caught and tossed out of class. Don't quit making payments; they will come and repossess your truck.

Most of those lessons are really silly, but I can tell you the deepest lessons I have ever learned have come on the business end of pain. C. S. Lewis said, "Pain removes the veil; it plants the flag of truth within the fortress of a rebel soul." I learned how to live one day at a time only after I nearly lost my family due to sinful choices. I learned that the path to intimacy is through humility and service to my wife only after almost losing the love of my life. I learned that I am a favored son of the living God and that is all I need for an identity, only after I lost my reputation in this world. I learned to be content in whatever state I'm in, only after I lost my career.

Pain has taught me the deepest and best lessons about what

it means to be a man. And yet, I avoid it these days at all costs. I eat ibuprofen like candy. I worship idols of comfort as if there were no God in heaven. I avoid conflict because I want to be liked. I watch reality TV so that I won't have to live in reality.

So, God comes along and splashes a little pain in my life: Like relational failures. Like professional set-backs. Like the creaks and groans of old age. Like breaking my leg doing the thing I love more than just about anything—backpacking.

If you are feeling pain in your life right now, would you hear a word from a veteran pain-warrior? Listen to the still small voice of the Holy Spirit and see if there might be a lesson in your pain. The lesson might be as simple as don't text while you drive. Or it might be as deep as don't use your vocation to validate your existence. But you won't know if you don't listen.

So, Pain and I wrestle. Sometimes it wins and I learn. Sometimes I win and medicate. When I medicate I only delay the pain and the lesson I need to learn. How arrogant of me to think that I can learn what it means to follow Jesus and not experience deep pain. Jesus never avoided pain. In fact, here is a little known verse about Jesus: "Though He was a Son, yet He learned obedience by the things which He suffered" (*New King James Version,* Heb. 5:8).

Bet you didn't know that.

Green Pastures

It has been said that 125 people died in World War II for every word of Hitler's *Mein Kampf*, a thick book of 720 pages. In a suicide note a teenage girl wrote, "They said...", then she took her life. Words can kill. I remember what a coach said to me about my body when I was a boy that causes me to be insecure until this day. Words can scar. The president can give a speech that causes the stock market to soar or tank. A dictator can boast of weapons of mass destruction and a war results. Words can influence.

As a pastor and a writer, I wrestle with words, and many days the words win. But I love words. I read the little bird tracks across paper and electronic books, write them longhand in my journal, and type them on this computer. I listen to them intoned by a professionally trained actor as he reads someone else's words and I speak them every Sunday morning. I listen to them every day in various coffee houses near where I live. I even speak a few caffeinated words myself. I love words. Words can be a balm or salve for a wounded heart. I love listening to them in a lover's ballad or even a protest song.

I can be transported to another planet when I read *Perelandra* or find myself in a dusty Texas border town called Lonesome Dove. I can laugh at the outrageous characters dreamed up by Flannery O'Connor or feel a tear track down my cheek at the last scene in *The Grapes of Wrath*. In so many ways words are my world. No words, however, written by great authors or spoken by skilled orators, compare with the Word of God to bring lasting change to a culture, guidance to a government, or gentle encouragement to a frightened heart.

Recently my wife and I visited an elderly saint in our church who was in the hospital with a broken hip. Her daughter was by her side and waved us in. After washing our hands we walked in, and when this frail octogenarian saw me, with tubes taped to her knobby hands, she reached for me. Holding her hand, I asked how she was and assured her of the prayer support of her church family. Her chest moved up and down, and a deep guttural rasp escaped with every exhale, as if she were pushing a piano off her chest with every breath. It was painful to watch and hear. There was a wild look of concern in the saint's eyes. What you might expect from someone who was uncertain about her next gasp of air.

Her daughter asked if I had a Bible. A little rise of embarrassment flushed my face as I said I didn't have my toolbox with me. She said the hospital couldn't find one and her mother wanted to read the 23rd Psalm. I said, "Well, I think I might be able to recite most of it. Would that be okay?" The saint nodded her head. Placing my right hand on her forehead and holding her hand with my left, I began to recite from a sketchy King James memory, "The Lord is my Shepherd; I shall not want." She closed her eyes and her breathing grew quiet and serene. I continued, "He maketh me to lie down in green pastures; he leadeth me beside the still waters. He restoreth my soul…" Her breathing now as gentle as a baby's, I looked at her daughter and tears were streaming down her face.

> He leadeth me in the paths of righteousness for His name's sake. Give us this day our daily bread. and Yea, though I walk through the shadow of death, I will fear no evil; for thou art with me; thy rod and thy staff they comfort me. Forgive us our trespasses as we forgive those who trespass against us. Surely mercy and goodness shall follow all the days of my life; For Thine is the Kingdom, the power, and the glory forever and ever. Amen.

I glanced at my wife and her head was cocked to one side like a puppy listening to a squeaky toy for the first time. I knew I had botched the recitation. The lady opened her eyes and looked at me. I asked, "Did that sound familiar?" With misty eyes she slowly nodded her head once and then her breathing became heavy and labored again. I tried to wrap up the visit so we wouldn't tire her out. She grasped my hand tightly and said, "Pastor, I have confessed all my sins to Jesus and I am ready to go." I smiled and said, "It's not time for that yet." She said, "Well, stay or go—either way, it's fine." Her words fell like notes from a lover's ballad to my heart. They reminded me of the Apostle Paul who said, "For me to live is Christ, and to die is gain." Words of love and longing. I would be so blessed to brim with such faith. May it be so in my life now, and when my day of labored breathing comes. I witnessed the power of the Word of God to transport a saint to a green pasture and still waters, if for only a moment, but she was ready for that pasture to be her home.

Am I so ready?

Seeing God

Persons rarely become present where they are not heartily wanted.

~ Dallas Willard

Do you remember the time when Moses was tending sheep in the wilderness of Sinai and saw a flickering fire off in the distance? Moses said, "What's going on here? I can't believe this! Amazing! Why doesn't the bush burn up?"

God saw that he had stopped to look and called to him from out of the bush, "Moses! Moses!"

Moses said, "Yes? I'm right here!"

God said, "Don't come any closer. Remove your sandals from your feet. You're standing on holy ground."

There are times in our walk with God in which we are confronted with the transcendent presence of the holy and we are undone; words seem trivial, actions seem futile. There is nothing to do but be quiet, be still. I fear we have begun to think of God as such a "buddy" and companion that we have lost the grandeur of His majesty. We have made God into such a democrat that we expect Him to be at our beck and call like some cosmic houseboy. I am aware of the fact that Jesus is our friend, brother, and boon companion, but may I also say that He is God, very God. There is an otherness about Him beyond our knowing. There is an over-and-aboveness about Him that exceeds our grasp. The only appropriate response to His presence is one of quiet humility.

When God spoke to Job asking if he was around when the worlds were spoken into existence, Job could do nothing but put his hand over his mouth. When confronted with the presence of God in the Temple, Isaiah could only say, "I am undone." When Peter went fishing with Jesus, he did not say, "Fish on!" He said, "Go away from me, Lord, for I am a sinful man." When Moses approached the fiery manifestation of God, he removed his shoes and later, he hid in the cleft of the rock as the backside of God passed by. A woman anointed Jesus's feet with her tears and wiped them with her flowing hair. A man approached Jesus and fell at His feet making his requests known to the Lord. Paul saw the resurrected Jesus on the road to Damascus and fell to the ground. There are places and spaces of holiness in this fallen world that demand an unusual posture from those who would follow Jesus.

What do you see? What do you hear? Annie Dillard in *Pilgrim at Tinker Creek*, says,

> I used to be able to see flying insects in the air. I'd look ahead and see, not the row of hemlocks across the road, but the air in front of it. My eyes would focus along that column of air, picking out flying insects. But I lost interest, I guess, for I dropped the habit. Now I can see birds.

Blaise Pascal worried that the biggest threat to the spiritual life for folks in his day was their relentless ability to distract themselves from thinking about God.

I was speaking with someone and said I wanted to live a life so compelling that my friends would want to walk closer with God. He stared at me. I could see that he was thinking about something, but I couldn't tell if the thoughts swirling in his head had anything to do with my statement. He looked down and his chin began to quiver. He stood up and walked a few feet and began to cry. At first just a few tears came, then a few more. No sound; then heavy sighs and inaudible moans, and soon with a full-on lament worthy of Jeremiah. I have witnessed a man weep like that about three times in my life; one of those was me. This went on for about five minutes—wailing. Instantly my pastor's heart was aroused to offer some comfort, but I couldn't tell if I wanted to comfort him so that he would feel better or that I would feel better. Is there anything more awkward than seeing a full-grown man weep?

I opened my mouth wanting to say: What's going on inside you? What are you feeling? Do you want to talk about the pain? How can I help you? Do you want to pray? I opened my mouth, but nothing came out. "Shut up," God said. So, in spite of my natural tendencies to insert my truncated wisdom where it is not invited, I kept my mouth shut. In time, he wiped his eyes on the sleeve of his brown shirt, blew his nose, cleared his throat, and apologized to me for his emotions. I said nothing. To this day I have no idea what was going on in that moment. What I do know is that I was to give him space—sacred space—to let that moment happen between him and God.

What do you see? What do you hear? I'm calling you to join me in refusing to be distracted by the white noise of this culture. We must slow down. We can't hear His voice if we are constantly checking social media, watching UN-reality TV, or playing video games. In order to see and hear, we have to be willing to say no to the siren song of cultural distractions and intend to pay attention.

You never know when you will find yourself on holy ground.

Watching for the King

Teaching some management courses on the Pine Ridge Indian reservation for the Little Wound School District a few years ago, I was impressed by their spirituality. Before one of the courses was about to begin, the leader asked one of the elders of the tribe, who happened to be the athletic director of the school, to lead in prayer. They pushed back from the tables and as we all stood, the elder Arlo Provost began to pray in Lakota. It took my breath away; I had no idea what he was saying, but I had never heard anything like it. He said, "Amen," then sat down and we all sat down too. I was stunned. Then they all turned their heads to me. I opened my notes and began to teach them about managing multiple priorities. I felt like the foreigner that I was.

It reminded me of a story I read somewhere that I hope is true about one of the rites of passage of Lakota boys. A father would take his son out into the wilderness at age fourteen and leave him there by himself overnight with scant provisions to survive the day and night. It is said the boy would spend most of the night sitting up listening to all the wild sounds of the night: the owls hooting, the rustling in the brush, the snorts in the dark, and the wolves howling. A very restless and frightful night for the young brave, but in the morning when the dawn would break over the eastern horizon, off about a hundred yards, the boy would see a lone man standing beside a tree. Then the man would start walking towards him, and the boy would recognize the walk of this warrior-father. He would have been there all night watching his son.

God is kind of like that with us. Sometimes I cry out to God, "God, where are you? I just don't see you!" And in that still, small voice God says, "Remember the Sunday School class

149

when the teacher, Mrs. Peggram, made you leave the class because she couldn't get you to shut up? That was Me. How about that time when your head hurt so badly that you cried yourself to sleep and your mom came to your room to rub your neck? That was Me. Remember when your dad came to give you a ride home when the meanest kid in school wanted to beat you up? I was there. I was caring for you.

"Remember when you were in high school, and you were gangly and awkward, and nobody wanted to be around you, and you felt all alone? You weren't. I was there. Remember when you were in college, and you were so empty because you thought I had gone away? And you even doubted that I existed? And you walked around that campus crying out, 'If you are here . . . show me'? I was there. I was right beside you. Remember when you were working construction and couldn't pay your bills, and they came and repossessed your truck? You cried yourself to sleep that night; I was there.

"Remember in your forties, when you lost your job, your friends, your sense of purpose, and you thought you were never going to see light again? I was right there. Remember when you stopped and ate lunch at that Burger King in Vernal, Utah, and told your oldest son why you lost your job and were leaving Colorado? I was there at the table with you and the next 200 miles of silence that hung between you and your fourteen-year-old son. Don't ask where I've been. I've been close the whole time."

I find meaning in paraphrasing a famous passage of scripture from the Old Testament. See if it speaks to you as well. Try placing your name where I have put mine.

> When Joe was a child, I loved him,
> And out of sin I called My son.
> But the more I called him,
> The more he ran from Me.
> He sacrificed to the gods of this world,
> And burned incense to carved images.

I taught little Joe to walk,
Taking him by his spindly arms;
But he did not know that I healed his wounds.
I drew him with gentle cords,
With bands of love,
I stooped and held him.

God is always near, redeeming, guiding, forming, mending, and protecting us.

Today, my oldest son celebrates the seventh anniversary of his marriage to my daughter-in-love, Ashley. This could not have happened had God not taken an active and sovereign role in the life I was trying to live. I don't understand how God uses past mistakes to make beautiful art, like a wonderful marriage of seven years for my son and his four redheaded angels, but He does.

As we live our lives, fretting about what goes bump in the night, keep your eyes on the eastern sky. One day, maybe not too distant from now, we will see our Warrior-King returning to wipe away every tear from our eyes, heal our wounds, and set things to rights in this sorry, dark world. We are not nearly as alone as we think we are. This is His promise. This is our hope.

"Amen. Even so, come, Lord Jesus," I say.

The Rescuer Was Rescued

Ministry that costs nothing, accomplishes nothing.

~ J.H. Jowett

Sometimes pain has rewards that transcend discomfort. Remember when I told you about my broken fibula? Well my rescuer was a young man named Boris, who volunteered for Search and Rescue. He was on a random day hike when he found me and radioed for a helicopter to come to our location. While we waited, we talked. I found out he was born in America and moved with his folks to the Netherlands when he was quite young; they divorced soon after that. He said he was going through a divorce.

The chopper arrived and I said goodbye. Later we connected on Facebook. Below is our first conversation:

September 13, 2011:

Boris,

I hope you are doing well. I think about you quite a bit as I mend with this broken leg. Thanks again for helping me up in the mountains. You were extremely professional. I felt completely safe and sound when you arrived and took control of my situation.

Regards,

joe

Joe,

I am doing well and I hope you are doing well too. Have they told you how long it will be before you can walk again?

Boris

End of story, right? Wrong. On Sunday, September 1, 2013, I stood up to preach in my church. It was two years to the day after Boris found me sprawled on the side of the mountain that I found him sitting in my church. I announced his presence to the congregation, and they gave him a hero's welcome. Boris didn't know it was the anniversary of the day he found me in the wilderness. I invited him to our house for Sunday lunch and asked him why he came to church today. He said many things, but one thing stood out to me. He said he was missing something in his life and wanted to explore Christianity. We made plans to go on a hike together later that week. Then he came to church again and we met for coffee and we talked further about issues that had hindered him from embracing faith in Jesus. It was after that coffee conversation that we exchanged the following Facebook conversation:

9/16/2013, 5:24 p.m.

Boris,

I really enjoyed our talk today. I want you to know that it means a lot to me that you desire to further your understanding of Christianity.

Just to be clear about what I heard you say today...you said you believe that God has been leading you to a closer walk with him since we met on the trail, your relationship with Hannah and then coming to church on the two-year anniversary, September 1. All of this has led you to believe that Jesus is calling you to Himself. Is that how you see it?

If so, like I've said to you before and again yesterday in my sermon, there is a time when a person is not a Christian and then they "convert" and commit their lives to Jesus and decide to follow him for the rest of their lives. They become an apprentice of Christ. Trusting in Him to forgive them of their sins and taking him at His word that He is the one and only Son of God.

I realize that is a very exclusive idea. But I didn't make it...Jesus did. So, I would ask you to step across the line and commit to Jesus by entering into a permanent covenant relationship with him. You can do that privately by praying a prayer. You can show that publicly by being baptized as a symbol of your new covenant relationship. Pray this prayer in your heart to God who hears the motives of our hearts:

"Dear God, I believe you sent your son, Jesus, to die for my sins so I can be forgiven. I'm sorry for my sins and I want to live the rest of my life the way you want me to. Please put your Spirit in my life to direct me. Amen."

If you prayed that prayer and meant it...you, Boris, are in God's forever family. I am your brother. The only thing next to do is find a lake, get dunked, and tell the church that Jesus is your Lord and Savior. After that we will walk together as brothers and I will teach you as best I can how to live out your faith as an apprentice of Jesus.

I am honored to be on this journey with you. Let me know if you understand this email and if you prayed the little prayer.

Your friend,
        joe

                                        9/16, 10:59 p.m.

Joe,

Yes you're right about all that. I think that God knows me, and he knows that I am very stubborn and self-sufficient. But he knows I am a good person and that ultimately I need him. So he has been trying very hard to lead me towards him. I have no doubt that, that day he sent me to Gothic Basin to find you. And just that alone is such a clear sign that I should have no doubts that Jesus is the way to reach him.

But I still didn't come to him, so he let me figure out my life on my own for a little longer.

I think the only thing that is holding me back is a fear for the unknown. I hate not knowing what's going to happen. What will happen…whether or not I will get this new job, whether or not I will be able to take time off to visit my family, whether or not…

The ultimate unknown is God. And with that I don't mean his existence. It's just that he is so much more than I can ever comprehend. No matter how much you study you will never know everything. So by entering in to a covenant relationship with him, you basically have to submit to the unknown and trust that what will happen is going to be right… which is not easy.

But I think it's the right thing to do and I want to.

I often have these random thoughts and about an hour before I drove to Starbucks to meet you, I thought this "The only way to discover the beauty that lays beyond your arm's reach, is to step outside your comfort zone".

So that said, I want to do this. I said the "little prayer" (and some more). I think the perfect place to get baptized is at Foggy Lake in Gothic Basin. That's where this all started after all and it's a very beautiful and special place to me (although the water is going to be really cold).

And thanks again for all your time and help,
  ~ Boris

Boris was baptized on September 19, 2013, at five thousand

155

feet above sea level. We stood in the alpine lake waist-deep in icy water and I recited words that I have said hundreds of times in my ministry, "I baptize you, my brother, in the name of the Father, Son, and the Holy Spirit," but this time my voice quivered not from cold, but from the mystery of how God accomplishes His will.

The rescuer had been rescued. And the pain was worth it

Coming Home

...when he came to himself...

~ Luke 15:17

*It is good to be between a ruined house
of bondage and a holy promised land.*

~ Leonard Cohen

Jesus tells a story about a father with two sons. One stays home on the family farm and the younger son takes his inheritance and leaves home. He leaves the predictable comfort of hearth and home. He is off to see the world and he is not looking back. And as the old King James Bible puts it, he "took his journey into a far country, and there wasted his substance with riotous living" (Luke 15:13).

My first post-pastorate job was tearing down a condemned house. An old lady had lived in the house for decades with her countless cats. Tearing down the condemned house was a metaphor of my life. I had spent years building a resume, reputation and career as a trustworthy man. But because of my arrogance and stupidity, I had seen my life abandoned and condemned.

With this little yellow house I had already dismantled and hauled off all of the outlying buildings and porch, and I had knocked down many of the non-load bearing walls. Now it was time to go after the bathroom. The vanity came out without much resistance, the sink as well. The only thing left was the tub and the toilet. I decided to deal with the toilet first.

I removed the tank, carried it out and threw it into my truck to take to the dump. I unbolted the bowl from the floor, but it wouldn't budge. Something—time, rust, secret glue, some malicious spirit—had corroded, sealed, or soldered the toilet bowl to the floor.

Finally, I wrapped my arms around the cold, slick and disgusting bowl and heaved with all the vein-popping effort I could find. It wouldn't budge. I was frustrated, sad and ashamed of myself.

I remembered that only two months before I was on the board of trustees of a major Christian organization. I was a former president of the second largest denomination in the state of Colorado. I was well respected and admired and successful in almost every way.

Now I was trying to tear a toilet out of an old cat-woman's house. I remember wondering, "How many times had the cat lady's bare butt sat on this seat I was hugging?" I fell back against the bathtub with the sharp smell of urine piercing my nostrils and began to weep, "Oh, God how did I get here?"

Louder than an audible voice I heard the Father say, "You are with Me and we are going to be just fine."

My chest heaved with sobs of pain and unmitigated joy. God was with me on the floor of the cat lady's bathroom. I mattered to him.

"Okay," I said.

I got up off that bathroom floor, went over to the house where my wife was preparing lunch, gave her a kiss and went back and took a sledgehammer to that toilet. And every day of repentance in the last 20 years is a day further from the filth of the far country and a day of bright joy walking with the Father.

Listen to a prodigal pastor: You matter to your Heavenly Father and He alone has the power to restore you to your proper place in the family of God.

The Third Book of God

My father could hear a little animal step,
Or a moth in the dark against the screen,
And every far sound called the listening out
Into places where the rest of us had never been.

~ William Stafford, *Listening*

Sometimes a person needs a story more than food to stay alive.

~ Barry Lopez

Not too long ago I went for a walk with a friend. We walked about three miles as the crow flies, but much further inside his story tracing back years and hundreds of miles. He dared to trust me with the ink-black darkness of sin and the pastel-dawn of restoration.

I remembered thinking, "This is his pearl of great price, be very careful with it." I held his story in my large hands--as if fragile. He felt safe enough to let me carry it for a while as we walked down a dirt road. Carrying another person's story is one of the most sacred things I have ever done and ever hope to do.

Inside their story is the essence of who they are, what they've done and what they aspire to become. Embedded in their story are the colors and contours of a life God is eroding, wind-carving, storming, and growing into a landscape in which He would walk in the cool of the day.

I was a witness to the artistry of a Creator-God at work in the story of my brother. Together he and God were finger-painting a messy and yet breath-taking landscape of redemption.

A doe scampered across the trail, golden aspen leaves gently

159

clattered like organic wind-chimes in the mountain air—on and on came his words of pain, loss, and heartache. There was a dryness to the mountain air, a sharp contrast to the tears tracking down the soul of my friend.

He spoke of an emotionally distant father, the suicide of a close friend, loneliness that comes from caring for people, angst about what is truly important in life, insecurity about his own value and worth, a job that went bad, pain…pain…pain…. And then temptation. And then sin.

With such tenderness these words came from my friend. It was beautiful to hear his story. Lyrical. His pain made the telling even more elegant, like listening to an oboe high above the symphony as it lingers before flowing to a crescendo. It doesn't seem to fit and yet you can't imagine the piece without it.

We stopped and sat on a gray log. He asked me to tell my story. Thus we shared something much deeper. We shared our souls. And in the sharing of that deeper part of our lives, we experienced the presence of the Holy Spirit on that bench and we were safe, warm and loved.

I ask myself why I love hearing stories from my brothers and sisters, and it occurred to me that when I am invited into the story of my brother, it is like looking into a reflecting pool. I see three wavy images--one is the emaciated skeletal mess I have made of my own life and one is the shining splendor of the creature I am becoming by the grace of Christ. And as I peer through the gossamer veil of the Holy Spirit, I see a third—the backside of God.

The ancient church fathers said that nature is the second book of God. Should I be so bold to say that there might be a third?

Tell me your story.

Epilogue

The Confluence of Love

If two lie down together, they will keep warm; but how can one be warm alone?

~ The Preacher

People who love one another can be silent together.

~ Dallas Willard,

"I'm going to go out and cut some wood."

"Want me to go with you?" she asked.

"That would be great."

Living in the mountains is something I have dreamed about for over forty years—and now that dream has come true at the foot of Mt. Princeton. I am in heaven. I step out on my deck at night and can see a million pin-pricks of light in the night sky. Like so many tiny holes to heaven. I can go for a walk and dodge prickly pairs, see antelope, and smell the gentle decay of fallen leaves in the river bottom.

I am living my dream. My wife is living my dream—not hers.

She is a city girl. She likes the close proximity of Hobby Lobby, The Dollar Tree and Costco. She likes the security of people she loves very close to her or within easy driving distance. She likes well-kept lawns, paved streets and stop

161

lights.

So what is she doing volunteering to step outside and hold logs while I cut them with a chainsaw? She isn't living her life. She is living life. A life she didn't choose. A life that is happening before us as we follow the calling of the Lord.

Nearly 34 years ago we entered a covenant together for better or worse and she is anything if not loyal to a promise. When we watch *The Lord of the Rings* film trilogy the character she most closely identifies with is Samwise Gamgee. If Frodo, the ring-bearer, must go into Mordor then Sam will follow. It is who he is.

It is who she is, too.

My hand was hung loosely over the arm of my chair as we were mindlessly watching one of our favorite shows and she slipped her hand inside of mine. We are living in the confluence of our lives—now that kids are grown and gone and grandkids are a thousand miles away. Our souls are knitting together. We are becoming one—our hearts are beating together.

Did you hear about the couple who had been married for 72 years and loved each other to the very end? The couple was hospitalized after a car accident just outside of Marshalltown, Iowa. They were given a shared room in the ICU where they held hands in adjacent beds.

At 3:38 pm on a Wednesday, Gordon's breathing stopped. Though he was no longer alive, his heart monitor continued to register a beat.

The nurse told Gordon and Norma's son, Dennis Yeager, that the monitor was beeping "because they're holding hands, and Norma's heart beat is going through him."

Norma died at 4:38 pm, exactly one hour later.

Even when we are cutting wood together or praying together over a meal, we are living in the confluence of our lives—together.

A long love in the same direction.

Dear Lord,

I am not a very good man, but I am getting better all the time. By Your touch and grace, I am changing. Your tools for my transformation are painful, comforting and completely adequate. I thank You for what You are teaching me and how You are relentless in Your dedication to making me like Jesus. I wish it didn't require so much pain. But the clay doesn't complain about the Potter's touch. It just complies. So, press against any part of me, Lord, that doesn't please You and I will be the better for it. Amen.

About the Author

Joe Chambers is pastor of Mountain Heights Baptist Church in Buena Vista, CO. He studied at Oklahoma Baptist University, completing a two-year certification program in Soul Care from the Potter's Inn Soul Care Institute and Fuller Seminary. Currently an apprentice with Anam Cara in Spiritual Direction. Living with his wife Lynette at the base of Mt. Princeton, Joe is an avid reader and writer, loves to tell stories and spend time in the wilderness.

Endorsements

"Joe invites the reader into the rugged terrain of a journey where one discovers a man who has plainly seen his own humanity, and has encountered the pursuit of a good and loving God. A craftsman storyteller and unapologetic lover of Jesus and people, Joe offers honesty and fierce hope to those who might be looking for a story that would tell of a God who is intimately present and involved in the brokenness and beauty of his people." — **Rachel Reed**, Spiritual Director, Anam Cara Ministries

"Joe is an inspirational speaker and writer as well as a seasoned pastor who writes of life experiences, and sees the handiwork of God in nature and life. As you read you feel like you are right there with him. I have known him for over fifty years, and he loves JESUS and loves people. I encourage you to read this book." — **Timothy Peggram**, Farmer in Wiggins, Colorado

"I've made my way – in reality, am making my way -- on the journey of life more slowly than many, it seems. Along the way, these notes from a friend have prodded me and pointed me toward a narrower, more necessary path than what I imagined for the trip. For the tears, rest and laughter they offer as traveling companions, I'm grateful." — **Cameron Crabtree**, Editor of the Northwest Baptist Witness

"In *Field Notes on the Jesus Way*, Chambers combines the poetry of life and nature with the scars of experience to mark the path for our own journey in Christ. His pastoral perspective helps us with self-evaluation. At the same time, his thoughtful reflection challenges us to keep moving up the mountain toward the summit." — **Jamie Greening**, Pastor and Author of *A Dream Within.*

"I've had the privilege of reading Joe's work and knowing him personally for years. He's the kind of friend everyone needs. His writing, like the man himself, exudes wisdom, grace, transparency, and a longing to be closer to and more like Jesus. Hearing from him, in person or in writing, is always edifying." — **Carl Kincaid**, Key Account Manager for a Pharmaceutical Company (aka A Bloodstained Israelite in Kansas City)